SYSTEM DESIGN INTERVIEW

300
QUESTIONS AND ANSWERS

PREPARE AND PASS

ROB BOTWRIGHT

Published by Rob Botwright
Library of Congress Cataloging-in-Publication Data
ISBN 978-1-83938-722-7
Cover design by Rizzo

Disclaimer

The contents of this book are based on extensive research and the best available historical sources. However, the author and publisher make no claims, promises, or guarantees about the accuracy, completeness, or adequacy of the information contained herein. The information in this book is provided on an "as is" basis, and the author and publisher disclaim any and all liability for any errors, omissions, or inaccuracies in the information or for any actions taken in reliance on such information. The opinions and views expressed in this book are those of the author and do not necessarily reflect the official policy or position of any organization or individual mentioned in this book. Any reference to specific people, places, or events is intended only to provide historical context and is not intended to defame or malign any group, individual, or entity. The information in this book is intended for educational and entertainment purposes only. It is not intended to be a substitute for professional advice or judgment. Readers are encouraged to conduct their own research and to seek professional advice where appropriate. Every effort has been made to obtain necessary permissions and acknowledgments for all images and other copyrighted material used in this book. Any errors or omissions in this regard are unintentional, and the author and publisher will correct them in future editions.

TABLE OF CONTENTS: SYSTEM DESIGN INTERVIEW: 300 QUESTIONS AND ANSWERS

5

Introduction

Welcome to "System Design Interview: 300 Questions and Answers - Prepare and Pass" – your comprehensive guide to mastering the intricacies of system design interviews. In today's tech-driven world, system design plays a crucial role in shaping the architecture of complex software systems, ensuring scalability, reliability, and efficiency. Aspiring engineers and seasoned professionals alike must possess a solid understanding of system design principles to excel in technical interviews and thrive in the fast-paced world of technology.

This book bundle is meticulously curated to provide you with a comprehensive resource for navigating the challenges of system design interviews. Whether you are preparing for interviews at top tech companies, seeking to advance your career, or simply aiming to deepen your knowledge in system design, this bundle offers a wealth of insights, strategies, and practice questions to help you succeed.

"System Design Interview: 300 Questions and Answers - Prepare and Pass" is structured to cover a wide range of topics, from foundational concepts to advanced techniques, ensuring that readers of all levels can benefit from its contents. Each chapter is crafted to delve into specific areas of system design, offering detailed explanations, practical examples, and hands-on exercises to reinforce learning and comprehension.

Throughout this bundle, you will explore essential topics such as scalability, distributed systems, database design, load balancing, caching strategies, fault tolerance, and much more. By combining theoretical knowledge with real-world scenarios and interview-style questions, this bundle equips you with the tools and strategies necessary to tackle system design interviews with confidence and precision.

Whether you are a software engineer, computer science student, or technology enthusiast, "System Design Interview: 300 Questions and Answers - Prepare and Pass" is your ultimate companion on the journey to mastering system design interviews. With dedication, practice, and the invaluable insights provided within these pages, you will be well-prepared to ace your next system design interview and embark on a successful career in the field of technology. Let's dive in and prepare to conquer the challenges ahead!

Chapter 1: Introduction to System Design Interviews

System design interviews serve as a crucial component in the process of technical evaluations within the realm of software engineering. These interviews gauge an individual's capacity to architect scalable, reliable, and efficient systems to tackle intricate real-world challenges. In a landscape where the demand for scalable software solutions is on the rise, mastering system design interviews stands as an imperative for aspiring engineers and professionals striving for career advancement.

System design interviews are distinct from traditional coding interviews, shifting the focus from algorithms and data structures to broader architectural concepts and problem-solving skills. Candidates are often presented with open-ended questions or real-world scenarios, where they are expected to demonstrate their ability to analyze requirements, make design decisions, and communicate effectively.

One of the primary objectives of system design interviews is to assess a candidate's proficiency in designing systems that can handle increasing workloads or growing amounts of data without compromising on performance or availability. To achieve this, candidates must possess a solid understanding of fundamental concepts such as scalability, distributed systems, database design, and caching strategies.

CLI commands play a significant role in system design interviews, particularly when it comes to deploying and managing various components of a system. For instance, provisioning servers, configuring databases, and deploying applications are common tasks that may require the use of CLI commands. In cloud environments like AWS or Google Cloud, commands such as **aws ec2 run-instances** or **gcloud compute instances create** are employed to launch new virtual machines, while **aws rds create-db-instance** or **gcloud sql instances create** may be used to set up database instances.

Another aspect of system design interviews involves assessing a candidate's ability to analyze trade-offs and make design decisions based on various constraints. This includes considerations such as performance, scalability, reliability, cost, and ease of maintenance. Candidates must be able to justify their design choices and explain how they address specific requirements while balancing competing priorities.

Effective communication is paramount in system design interviews, as candidates are expected to articulate their thoughts clearly, explain their design rationale, and collaborate with interviewers to explore different design options. This includes being able to discuss complex technical concepts in a concise and understandable manner and being receptive to feedback and suggestions.

Preparing for system design interviews requires a multifaceted approach, including studying fundamental concepts, practicing problem-solving techniques, and gaining hands-on experience with designing and implementing real-world systems. Candidates can leverage resources such as books, online courses, practice problems, and mock interviews to sharpen their skills and build confidence.

In summary, system design interviews represent a critical stage in the evaluation process for software engineering roles, focusing on assessing candidates' ability to architect scalable and reliable systems. By mastering fundamental concepts, practicing problem-solving skills, and honing communication abilities, candidates can increase their chances of success in system design interviews and excel in their careers.

Chapter 2: Understanding Scalability

Q1: What is scalability in the context of system design interviews?

A1: Scalability refers to the ability of a system to handle increasing workloads or growing amounts of data without sacrificing performance or availability. It's a crucial consideration in system design interviews, where candidates are often asked to design architectures that can scale effectively to meet the needs of expanding user bases or growing datasets.

Q2: What are some key strategies for achieving scalability in system design?

A2: Some key strategies for achieving scalability include horizontal scaling (scaling out), which involves adding more resources, such as servers or instances, to distribute the workload across multiple machines. Another approach is vertical scaling (scaling up), which involves increasing the capacity of individual resources, such as upgrading to more powerful servers. Additionally, techniques such as caching, load balancing, and database sharding can help distribute and manage resources efficiently.

Q3: How do CLI commands play a role in achieving scalability?

A3: CLI commands are often used to provision and manage resources in scalable architectures. For example, in cloud environments, commands such as **aws ec2 run-instances** or **gcloud compute instances create** can be used to launch new virtual machines, while **aws elb create-load-balancer** or **gcloud compute backend-services create** can be used to set up load balancers. CLI commands streamline the process of deploying and scaling infrastructure components as needed.

Q4: Why is understanding scalability important in system design interviews?

A4: Understanding scalability is important in system design interviews because it demonstrates a candidate's ability to design systems that can accommodate growth and handle increasing demands effectively. Interviewers often assess a candidate's scalability considerations, including how they distribute workloads, manage resources, and plan for future growth. Demonstrating a deep understanding of scalability principles can set candidates apart in system design interviews.

Chapter 3: Database Design Fundamentals

Q1: What are some key considerations in database design for system design interviews?

A1: In system design interviews, candidates are often evaluated based on their understanding of database design fundamentals. This includes considerations such as data modeling, schema design, indexing strategies, normalization vs. denormalization, and choosing appropriate database technologies based on use cases and requirements.

Q2: How do database design decisions impact system scalability and performance?

A2: Database design decisions have a significant impact on system scalability and performance. For example, choosing the right data model and indexing strategy can improve query performance and reduce response times, while denormalization can help optimize read-heavy workloads. However, these decisions may also affect scalability, as denormalization can lead to data duplication and increase storage requirements.

Q3: What role do CLI commands play in database design for system design interviews?

A3: CLI commands are often used to manage database instances, configure schema, and perform administrative tasks in system design interviews. For instance, commands such as **CREATE TABLE, ALTER TABLE**, and **CREATE INDEX** are commonly used to define database schema and optimize performance. Additionally, commands for database backup, restoration, and monitoring are essential for ensuring data integrity and availability.

Q4: Why is a deep understanding of database design fundamentals important for system design interviews?

A4: A deep understanding of database design fundamentals is crucial for system design interviews because databases are at the core of many software systems. Interviewers often assess candidates based on their ability to design efficient and scalable database schemas, optimize query performance, and make informed decisions about data storage and retrieval. Demonstrating proficiency in database design can showcase a candidate's ability to architect robust and reliable systems.

Chapter 4: Distributed Systems

Q1: What are distributed systems, and why are they important in system design interviews?

A1: Distributed systems consist of multiple interconnected nodes that work together to achieve a common goal. They are crucial in system design interviews because they allow for scalable, fault-tolerant, and efficient architectures. Candidates are often evaluated based on their understanding of distributed system concepts such as consensus protocols, replication strategies, and communication protocols.

Q2: How do you ensure data consistency in distributed systems, and why is it challenging?

A2: Ensuring data consistency in distributed systems is challenging due to factors such as network partitions, latency, and node failures. Candidates may be asked about techniques such as distributed transactions, quorum-based consistency models, and conflict resolution strategies. They must demonstrate an understanding of trade-offs between consistency, availability, and partition tolerance (CAP theorem) in distributed systems.

Q3: What are some common scalability challenges in distributed systems, and how can they be addressed?

A3: Scalability challenges in distributed systems include bottlenecks in communication, resource contention, and coordination overhead. Candidates may be expected to discuss techniques such as sharding, partitioning, and load balancing to distribute and manage resources effectively. They should also be able to explain how these techniques help mitigate scalability challenges and improve system performance.

Q4: How do distributed systems handle fault tolerance, and what strategies can be employed to ensure system reliability?

A4: Distributed systems employ various strategies to handle faults and failures, including redundancy, replication, and error detection and recovery mechanisms. Candidates may be asked about techniques such as leader election, consensus algorithms (e.g., Paxos, Raft), and distributed consensus protocols (e.g., Two-Phase Commit, Three-Phase Commit). They should demonstrate an understanding of how these strategies contribute to system reliability and fault tolerance.

Chapter 5: Load Balancing Techniques

Q1: What is load balancing, and why is it essential in system design interviews?

A1: Load balancing is the process of distributing incoming network traffic across multiple servers to ensure optimal resource utilization, maximize throughput, and minimize response times. It is crucial in system design interviews because it helps candidates demonstrate their understanding of scalability, fault tolerance, and efficient resource allocation in distributed systems.

Q2: What are some common load balancing techniques used in distributed systems?

A2: Common load balancing techniques include round-robin DNS, weighted round-robin, least connections, IP hash, and least response time. Candidates may also be expected to discuss more advanced techniques such as dynamic load balancing, content-aware routing, and adaptive load balancing algorithms that take into account server health and workload characteristics.

Q3: How do you implement load balancing in practice, and what role do CLI commands play?

A3: Load balancing can be implemented using dedicated load balancer appliances or software-based load balancers deployed on servers or within cloud environments. CLI commands are often used to configure and manage load balancers, including tasks such as creating load balancer pools, configuring health checks, and adding or removing backend servers. For example, in AWS, commands such as **aws elb create-load-balancer** and **aws elb register-instances-with-load-balancer** are used to set up and manage Elastic Load Balancers.

Q4: What considerations should be taken into account when designing a load balancing strategy for a system?

A4: When designing a load balancing strategy, candidates should consider factors such as traffic patterns, server capacity, geographic distribution of users, and application-specific requirements. They should also assess the trade-offs between different load balancing algorithms in terms of simplicity, scalability, and performance. Additionally, candidates should plan for redundancy and fault tolerance to ensure that the load balancer itself does not become a single point of failure in the system.

Chapter 6: Caching Strategies

Q1: What is caching, and why is it important in system design interviews?

A1: Caching is the process of storing frequently accessed data in a temporary storage layer to reduce latency, improve performance, and minimize the load on backend systems. It is crucial in system design interviews because it allows candidates to demonstrate their understanding of optimization techniques, scalability, and trade-offs in designing efficient systems.

Q2: What are some common caching strategies used in distributed systems?

A2: Common caching strategies include in-memory caching using technologies like Memcached or Redis, content delivery networks (CDNs) for caching static content closer to users, and browser caching for storing resources locally on client devices. Candidates may also discuss techniques such as cache sharding, cache invalidation, and time-to-live (TTL) expiration policies to manage cache consistency and eviction.

Q3: How do you determine what data to cache and for how long?

A3: The decision of what data to cache and for how long depends on factors such as data access patterns, data volatility, and application requirements. Candidates may use techniques such as profiling and monitoring to identify frequently accessed data and measure cache hit rates. They should also consider trade-offs between cache size, cache freshness, and cache invalidation strategies to optimize cache effectiveness.

Q4: How do you implement caching in practice, and what role do CLI commands play?

A4: Caching can be implemented using caching libraries or frameworks integrated into application code, caching servers deployed as standalone services, or managed caching solutions provided by cloud providers. CLI commands are often used to deploy and manage caching infrastructure, configure caching parameters, and monitor cache performance. For example, in Redis, commands such as **redis-cli set** and **redis-cli get** are used to set and retrieve cache data, while **redis-cli info** provides insights into cache metrics and statistics.

Chapter 7: Message Queues and Event Sourcing

Q1: What are message queues, and why are they important in system design interviews?

A1: Message queues are intermediary components that facilitate communication between different parts of a system by storing, routing, and delivering messages asynchronously. They are crucial in system design interviews because they enable decoupling, scalability, and fault tolerance in distributed systems. Candidates are often evaluated based on their understanding of message queue architectures, patterns, and use cases.

Q2: What are some common message queue implementations used in distributed systems?

A2: Common message queue implementations include Apache Kafka, RabbitMQ, Amazon SQS (Simple Queue Service), and Redis Pub/Sub. Each of these implementations offers different features and trade-offs in terms of scalability, durability, message ordering, and delivery guarantees. Candidates may be expected to discuss the strengths and limitations of different message queue technologies and select appropriate solutions based on specific requirements.

Q3: How does event sourcing differ from traditional database-centric architectures, and why is it relevant in system design interviews?

A3: Event sourcing is a pattern where system state changes are captured as a series of immutable events, which are stored and replayed to reconstruct the current state of the system. It differs from traditional database-centric architectures, where only the current state is stored in a mutable database. Event sourcing is relevant in system design interviews because it offers benefits such as auditability, scalability, and flexibility in designing event-driven architectures.

Q4: How do you ensure message durability and reliability in distributed systems using message queues?

A4: Ensuring message durability and reliability in distributed systems involves techniques such as persistent message storage, message acknowledgment, and message replication. Candidates may discuss strategies such as configuring message queue persistence, implementing message acknowledgments, and setting up message retry mechanisms to handle failures and ensure message delivery guarantees. Additionally, they should consider designing idempotent message processing logic to handle duplicate messages and ensure system consistency.

Chapter 8: Designing for Fault Tolerance

Q1: What is fault tolerance, and why is it important in system design interviews?

A1: Fault tolerance refers to a system's ability to continue operating properly in the event of component failures. It's crucial in system design interviews because it demonstrates a candidate's understanding of designing robust and reliable systems that can withstand failures without causing disruptions to the overall functionality.

Q2: What are some common techniques for designing fault-tolerant systems?

A2: Common techniques for designing fault-tolerant systems include redundancy, replication, graceful degradation, and failure detection and recovery mechanisms. Candidates may also discuss strategies such as implementing health checks, automatic failover, and load balancing to maintain system availability and resilience in the face of failures.

Q3: How do you implement fault tolerance in practice, and what role do CLI commands play?

A3: Implementing fault tolerance involves deploying redundant components, monitoring system health, and automating failure recovery processes. CLI commands play a role in managing and configuring fault-tolerant components, such as setting up redundant servers, configuring automatic failover policies, and monitoring system metrics. For example, in a cloud environment, commands such as **aws autoscaling create-auto-scaling-group** and **aws elb configure-health-check** can be used to set up auto-scaling groups and configure health checks for load balancers.

Q4: Why is designing for fault tolerance considered a trade-off in system design?

A4: Designing for fault tolerance often involves trade-offs in terms of complexity, cost, and performance. For example, adding redundancy and replication can increase infrastructure costs and complexity, while implementing automatic failover mechanisms may introduce additional latency and overhead. Candidates must weigh these trade-offs and make informed decisions based on specific requirements and constraints to achieve an optimal balance between fault tolerance and other system attributes.

Chapter 9: Consistency and Availability Trade-offs

Q1: What are consistency and availability trade-offs in system design, and why are they important to consider?

A1: Consistency and availability trade-offs refer to the dilemma of achieving strong consistency guarantees while maintaining high availability in distributed systems. It's crucial to consider these trade-offs in system design interviews because they require candidates to make informed decisions about data consistency models, replication strategies, and fault tolerance mechanisms to balance between consistency and availability based on application requirements and use cases.

Q2: What are some common consistency models used in distributed systems?

A2: Common consistency models include strong consistency, eventual consistency, and causal consistency. Strong consistency guarantees that all nodes see the same data at the same time, while eventual consistency allows for temporary inconsistencies that eventually converge. Causal consistency ensures that causally related operations are ordered correctly. Candidates may discuss the strengths and limitations of each consistency model and choose appropriate models based on application requirements.

Q3: How do you achieve consistency and availability trade-offs in distributed databases?

A3: Achieving consistency and availability trade-offs in distributed databases involves implementing techniques such as replication, partitioning, and quorum-based consistency models. Candidates may discuss strategies such as choosing the appropriate replication factor, configuring consistency levels (e.g., strong consistency vs. eventual consistency), and implementing conflict resolution mechanisms to balance between consistency and availability based on system requirements.

Q4: Why is understanding the CAP theorem important in designing distributed systems?

A4: The CAP (Consistency, Availability, Partition tolerance) theorem states that in a distributed system, it's impossible to simultaneously achieve strong consistency, high availability, and partition tolerance. Understanding the CAP theorem is important in system design interviews because it helps candidates grasp the inherent trade-offs between consistency, availability, and partition tolerance in distributed systems. Candidates must demonstrate their ability to make design decisions that prioritize one aspect over others based on application requirements and constraints.

Chapter 10: System Design for Web Applications

Q1: What are the key considerations when designing web applications in system design interviews?

A1: When designing web applications in system design interviews, candidates need to consider various factors such as scalability, performance, security, and user experience. They must demonstrate an understanding of front-end and back-end architecture, data storage, caching strategies, load balancing, and fault tolerance mechanisms to ensure a robust and efficient web application design.

Q2: How do you ensure scalability in the architecture of web applications?

A2: Scalability in web application architecture can be achieved through horizontal scaling, vertical scaling, or a combination of both. Candidates may discuss techniques such as load balancing, caching, database sharding, and microservices architecture to distribute and manage resources effectively and accommodate growing user bases and traffic loads.

Q3: What security considerations should be taken into account when designing web applications?

A3: Security is a critical aspect of web application design, and candidates must address considerations such as authentication, authorization, data validation, encryption, and protection against common security threats such as SQL injection, cross-site scripting (XSS), and cross-site request forgery (CSRF). They should also discuss best practices for securing communication channels, implementing access controls, and regularly auditing and updating security measures to mitigate potential risks.

Q4: How do you optimize performance in web application design?

A4: Optimizing performance in web application design involves various techniques such as minimizing latency, reducing bandwidth usage, optimizing database queries, and leveraging caching mechanisms. Candidates may also discuss strategies such as content delivery networks (CDNs), asynchronous processing, lazy loading, and client-side optimizations to improve page load times, responsiveness, and overall user experience.

Chapter 11: Microservices Architecture

Q1: What is microservices architecture, and why is it relevant in system design interviews?

A1: Microservices architecture is an approach to designing software systems as a collection of loosely coupled, independently deployable services, each responsible for a specific business function. It's relevant in system design interviews because it allows candidates to demonstrate their understanding of scalability, modularity, fault tolerance, and deployment strategies in distributed systems.

Q2: What are the key advantages of using microservices architecture?

A2: Some key advantages of microservices architecture include improved scalability, flexibility, and agility, as services can be developed, deployed, and scaled independently. It also enables better fault isolation, faster release cycles, and easier maintenance and updates compared to monolithic architectures. Candidates may discuss how microservices promote team autonomy, technology diversity, and continuous delivery practices.

Q3: What challenges are associated with implementing microservices architecture?

A3: Implementing microservices architecture introduces challenges such as service communication, data consistency, distributed tracing, and operational complexity. Candidates may discuss strategies for managing service dependencies, ensuring transactional consistency across services, implementing service discovery and load balancing, and monitoring and troubleshooting distributed systems effectively.

Q4: How do you design a microservices architecture for a web application?

A4: Designing a microservices architecture for a web application involves identifying and decomposing business functionalities into separate services, defining service boundaries, and establishing communication protocols between services. Candidates may discuss principles such as single responsibility, loose coupling, and high cohesion to guide service design decisions. They should also consider factors such as service granularity, data partitioning, and deployment strategies to optimize performance, scalability, and maintainability.

Chapter 12: Designing for Performance

Q1: Why is designing for performance crucial in system design interviews?

A1: Designing for performance is critical in system design interviews because it demonstrates a candidate's ability to create efficient and responsive systems that meet user expectations and business requirements. Performance considerations encompass various aspects, including response times, throughput, latency, and resource utilization, all of which impact user experience and system scalability.

Q2: What are some common performance bottlenecks in system design, and how can they be mitigated?

A2: Common performance bottlenecks include slow database queries, inefficient algorithms, network latency, and resource contention. Candidates may discuss strategies such as optimizing database indexes, caching frequently accessed data, minimizing network round-trips, and using asynchronous processing to mitigate bottlenecks and improve system performance.

Q3: How do you measure and analyze performance in system design interviews?

A3: Measuring and analyzing performance involves techniques such as profiling, benchmarking, and monitoring system metrics. Candidates may discuss tools and methodologies for identifying performance bottlenecks, measuring response times, and analyzing resource utilization. They should also demonstrate an understanding of performance testing techniques, including load testing, stress testing, and capacity planning, to ensure systems can handle expected workloads.

Q4: What role does caching play in designing for performance, and how can it be effectively utilized?

A4: Caching plays a crucial role in improving performance by reducing latency and minimizing the load on backend systems. Candidates may discuss caching strategies such as in-memory caching, content delivery networks (CDNs), and browser caching to cache static content and frequently accessed data closer to users. They should also consider cache invalidation strategies, expiration policies, and cache eviction algorithms to ensure cache consistency and maximize performance benefits.

Chapter 13: Data Partitioning Techniques

Q1: What are data partitioning techniques, and why are they important in system design interviews?

A1: Data partitioning techniques involve splitting datasets into smaller partitions or shards to distribute storage and processing across multiple nodes in a distributed system. They are important in system design interviews because they allow candidates to demonstrate their understanding of scalability, performance, and fault tolerance in large-scale data systems.

Q2: What are some common data partitioning strategies used in distributed databases?

A2: Common data partitioning strategies include range partitioning, hash partitioning, and key-based partitioning. Range partitioning involves dividing data based on ranges of values, while hash partitioning distributes data based on hash values of keys. Key-based partitioning assigns data to partitions based on specific keys or attributes. Candidates may discuss trade-offs between these strategies in terms of data distribution, query performance, and load balancing.

Q3: How do you choose the appropriate data partitioning strategy for a given application?

A3: Choosing the appropriate data partitioning strategy depends on factors such as data access patterns, query requirements, and scalability goals. Candidates may consider characteristics of the dataset, such as data skewness, access frequency, and distribution patterns, to inform their decision. They should also evaluate trade-offs between partitioning strategies, including partition size, query parallelism, and data redistribution complexity, to select the most suitable approach.

Q4: What challenges are associated with implementing data partitioning in distributed systems?

A4: Implementing data partitioning in distributed systems introduces challenges such as data skew, hotspots, and consistency management. Candidates may discuss strategies for handling uneven data distribution, mitigating hotspots through load balancing, and ensuring consistency across partitions using techniques such as distributed transactions or eventual consistency. They should also consider factors such as partitioning granularity, partition size, and partitioning key selection to optimize performance and scalability.

Chapter 14: Security Considerations in System Design

Q1: Why are security considerations crucial in system design interviews?

A1: Security considerations are crucial in system design interviews because they demonstrate a candidate's ability to design systems that protect against threats, vulnerabilities, and attacks. Security encompasses various aspects, including authentication, authorization, encryption, data protection, and compliance with regulatory standards, all of which are essential for safeguarding sensitive information and ensuring system integrity and trustworthiness.

Q2: What are some common security threats and vulnerabilities that system designers need to address?

A2: Common security threats and vulnerabilities include unauthorized access, injection attacks (e.g., SQL injection, cross-site scripting), broken authentication, sensitive data exposure, insecure direct object references, and security misconfigurations. Candidates may discuss techniques such as threat modeling, risk assessment, and security testing to identify and mitigate potential security risks throughout the system lifecycle.

Q3: How do you design authentication and authorization mechanisms for a system?

A3: Designing authentication and authorization mechanisms involves implementing techniques such as multi-factor authentication, OAuth, OpenID Connect, and role-based access control (RBAC). Candidates may discuss strategies for securely storing and managing user credentials, enforcing access controls based on user roles and permissions, and auditing and logging access activities to detect and respond to unauthorized behavior.

Q4: What role does encryption play in system design, and how can it be effectively implemented?

A4: Encryption plays a critical role in protecting data confidentiality and integrity in transit and at rest. Candidates may discuss techniques such as symmetric encryption, asymmetric encryption, and hashing to encrypt sensitive data, secure communication channels, and validate data integrity. They should also consider factors such as key management, encryption algorithms, and cryptographic protocols to ensure robust encryption practices and compliance with security standards.

Chapter 15: Designing APIs and Protocols

Q1: Why is designing APIs and protocols important in system design interviews?

A1: Designing APIs and protocols is essential in system design interviews because it involves defining communication interfaces and standards that enable interaction between different components of a system. APIs and protocols facilitate interoperability, modularity, and extensibility, allowing systems to evolve independently and integrate with third-party services seamlessly.

Q2: What are some key considerations when designing APIs for a system?

A2: When designing APIs, candidates need to consider factors such as usability, consistency, versioning, security, and performance. They should define clear and intuitive interfaces with well-documented endpoints, request/response formats, and error handling mechanisms. Additionally, candidates may discuss strategies for versioning APIs, implementing authentication and authorization mechanisms, and optimizing API performance through caching and pagination.

Q3: How do you design protocols for efficient communication between distributed components?

A3: Designing protocols involves defining rules and conventions for communication between distributed components, including message formats, transport protocols, and error handling mechanisms. Candidates may discuss techniques such as using RESTful principles for web APIs, defining message schemas with JSON or Protocol Buffers, and choosing appropriate transport protocols (e.g., HTTP, TCP, UDP) based on reliability, latency, and throughput requirements.

Q4: What role does API documentation play in system design, and how can it be effectively managed?

A4: API documentation is crucial for ensuring that developers understand how to use and interact with APIs effectively. Candidates may discuss best practices for documenting APIs, including providing clear and concise descriptions of endpoints, parameters, and response codes, along with examples and usage guidelines. They should also consider tools and platforms for generating and maintaining API documentation, such as Swagger/OpenAPI, Postman, or custom documentation portals.

Chapter 16: Real-time Data Processing

Q1: What is real-time data processing, and why is it important in system design interviews?

A1: Real-time data processing involves analyzing and acting on data as it is generated or received, without delay. It's crucial in system design interviews because it demonstrates a candidate's ability to design systems capable of handling and processing high-volume, time-sensitive data streams efficiently. Real-time data processing is essential in applications such as fraud detection, monitoring, recommendation systems, and IoT.

Q2: What are some common technologies and frameworks used for real-time data processing?

A2: Common technologies and frameworks for real-time data processing include Apache Kafka, Apache Flink, Apache Spark Streaming, and Apache Storm. These platforms provide capabilities for ingesting, processing, and analyzing streaming data in real-time, enabling applications to react quickly to changing data and generate timely insights. Candidates may discuss the strengths and trade-offs of each technology in different use cases.

Q3: How do you design a real-time data processing pipeline?

A3: Designing a real-time data processing pipeline involves defining data sources, ingestion mechanisms, processing logic, and output destinations. Candidates may discuss architectural patterns such as event sourcing, stream processing, and lambda architectures to handle data streams efficiently. They should also consider factors such as data partitioning, fault tolerance, and scalability when designing pipelines for processing large-scale data in real-time.

Q4: What challenges are associated with implementing real-time data processing systems?

A4: Implementing real-time data processing systems introduces challenges such as data consistency, latency management, fault tolerance, and state management. Candidates may discuss strategies for ensuring data consistency across distributed components, managing processing delays and out-of-order data, implementing fault recovery mechanisms, and handling stateful computations in stateless environments. They should also consider trade-offs between consistency, availability, and partition tolerance in distributed systems to design robust and reliable real-time data processing pipelines.

Chapter 17: Content Delivery Networks (CDNs)

Q1: What is a Content Delivery Network (CDN), and why is it important in system design interviews?

A1: A Content Delivery Network (CDN) is a distributed network of servers that deliver web content to users based on their geographic location, reducing latency and improving performance. It's important in system design interviews because CDNs help optimize content delivery, enhance user experience, and scale infrastructure to handle high volumes of traffic efficiently.

Q2: What are the key benefits of using a Content Delivery Network (CDN) in web applications?

A2: Some key benefits of using a CDN include improved website performance, reduced latency, increased reliability, and enhanced security. CDNs cache static content and serve it from edge servers located closer to end-users, reducing the distance data travels and improving load times. Additionally, CDNs provide features such as DDoS protection, SSL/TLS termination, and content optimization to enhance security and scalability.

Q3: How do you integrate a Content Delivery Network (CDN) into a web application architecture?

A3: Integrating a CDN into a web application architecture involves configuring DNS settings, configuring caching rules, and optimizing content delivery. Candidates may discuss techniques such as using a CDN provider's API or CDN-as-a-Service solutions to automate deployment and management tasks. They should also consider factors such as cache invalidation strategies, purging stale content, and measuring CDN performance to optimize content delivery.

Q4: What considerations should be taken into account when selecting a Content Delivery Network (CDN) provider?

A4: When selecting a CDN provider, candidates should consider factors such as geographic coverage, network performance, reliability, security features, pricing, and support. They may evaluate CDN providers based on their global network infrastructure, edge server locations, integration capabilities with existing systems, and ability to meet specific performance and scalability requirements. Additionally, candidates may consider CDN features such as HTTP/2 support, TLS termination, and real-time analytics to enhance content delivery and user experience.

Chapter 18: Designing for High Availability

Q1: What is high availability, and why is it important in system design interviews?

A1: High availability refers to the ability of a system to remain operational and accessible for users, typically measured as a percentage of uptime over a given period. It's crucial in system design interviews because it demonstrates a candidate's understanding of designing resilient and reliable systems that minimize downtime and ensure continuous service availability, even in the face of failures or disruptions.

Q2: What are some common strategies for designing high availability systems?

A2: Common strategies for designing high availability systems include redundancy, fault tolerance, load balancing, and disaster recovery planning. Candidates may discuss techniques such as deploying multiple instances across geographically distributed regions, using load balancers to distribute traffic evenly, implementing automatic failover mechanisms, and replicating data across redundant storage systems to minimize single points of failure and ensure continuous operation.

Q3: How do you measure and monitor system availability in real-time?

A3: Measuring and monitoring system availability involves using metrics such as uptime, downtime, mean time between failures (MTBF), mean time to recover (MTTR), and service level agreements (SLAs) to assess system reliability and performance. Candidates may discuss tools and techniques for monitoring system health, such as logging, alerting, and performance monitoring systems, to detect and respond to issues proactively and ensure high availability and service quality.

Q4: What challenges are associated with designing for high availability, and how can they be addressed?

A4: Designing for high availability introduces challenges such as complexity, cost, and trade-offs between availability, consistency, and performance. Candidates may discuss strategies for mitigating these challenges, such as designing for fault tolerance, implementing redundancy at various levels of the system architecture, and automating recovery procedures to minimize downtime. They should also consider factors such as scalability, data consistency, and disaster recovery planning to ensure that high availability designs are robust, scalable, and resilient to failures.

Chapter 19: Case Studies in System Design

Q1: What are case studies in system design, and why are they important in system design interviews?

A1: Case studies in system design involve analyzing real-world scenarios or problems and designing solutions based on specific requirements and constraints. They are important in system design interviews because they allow candidates to demonstrate their problem-solving skills, domain knowledge, and ability to apply design principles and best practices to practical scenarios.

Q2: How do you approach solving a case study in system design?

A2: When approaching a case study in system design, candidates should start by understanding the problem statement, defining requirements, and identifying key system components and interactions. They should then propose a high-level architecture, discuss trade-offs, and justify design decisions based on scalability, performance, reliability, and other relevant factors. Finally, candidates should outline implementation details, deployment strategies, and potential challenges or considerations.

Q3: What are some common types of case studies in system design interviews?

A3: Common types of case studies in system design interviews include designing social media platforms, e-commerce websites, content delivery networks (CDNs), ride-sharing applications, and messaging systems. Each case study presents unique challenges and considerations related to scalability, concurrency, data consistency, user experience, security, and other aspects of system design.

Q4: How do you evaluate the effectiveness of a solution proposed in a case study?

A4: Evaluating the effectiveness of a solution proposed in a case study involves assessing its alignment with requirements, feasibility, scalability, performance, reliability, and other relevant criteria. Interviewers may evaluate candidates based on their ability to articulate design decisions, justify trade-offs, and address potential challenges or limitations of the proposed solution. Candidates may also be asked to discuss alternative approaches or optimizations to further improve the proposed design.

Chapter 20: Optimization Strategies

Q1: What are optimization strategies in system design, and why are they important in interviews?

A1: Optimization strategies in system design involve techniques to improve system performance, efficiency, and resource utilization. They are crucial in interviews because they demonstrate a candidate's ability to identify bottlenecks, analyze trade-offs, and apply optimization techniques to enhance system scalability, reliability, and user experience.

Q2: What are some common areas where optimization is typically applied in system design?

A2: Optimization can be applied to various areas in system design, including database queries, algorithm efficiency, network communication, caching mechanisms, and resource allocation. Candidates may discuss techniques such as indexing, query optimization, algorithmic improvements, parallel processing, and compression to optimize system performance and throughput.

Q3: How do you approach optimizing a system design?

A3: When optimizing a system design, candidates should start by identifying performance bottlenecks and areas for improvement through profiling, monitoring, and performance testing. They should then prioritize optimizations based on their impact on critical system metrics, such as response time, throughput, and resource utilization. Candidates may iteratively apply optimization techniques, measure their effectiveness, and fine-tune the design to achieve desired performance goals.

Q4: What trade-offs should be considered when applying optimization strategies?

A4: When applying optimization strategies, candidates should consider trade-offs between performance, scalability, complexity, and maintainability. For example, optimizing database queries may involve adding indexes to improve read performance but may impact write performance and increase storage requirements. Similarly, optimizing caching mechanisms may improve response times but may introduce cache invalidation complexities and memory overhead. Candidates should evaluate trade-offs carefully and make informed decisions based on system requirements and constraints.

Chapter 21: System Design for Mobile Applications

Q1: What are the key considerations when designing systems for mobile applications?

A1: Designing systems for mobile applications involves considerations such as performance, network constraints, device compatibility, and offline capabilities. Candidates should focus on optimizing user experience, minimizing data usage, and ensuring seamless connectivity across different network conditions and device types.

Q2: How do you address performance challenges in mobile application design?

A2: Addressing performance challenges in mobile application design requires optimizing app size, reducing network requests, and minimizing CPU and battery usage. Candidates may discuss techniques such as lazy loading, image compression, code minification, and background processing to improve app responsiveness and resource efficiency.

Q3: What are some strategies for ensuring data efficiency in mobile applications?

A3: Ensuring data efficiency in mobile applications involves minimizing data transfer, optimizing data synchronization, and caching frequently accessed content locally. Candidates may discuss techniques such as data compression, delta updates, offline data storage, and prefetching to reduce data usage and improve app responsiveness, especially in bandwidth-constrained environments.

Q4: How do you design mobile applications to support offline usage?

A4: Designing mobile applications to support offline usage involves implementing local data storage, offline synchronization, and conflict resolution mechanisms. Candidates may discuss strategies such as using SQLite databases, implementing background synchronization tasks, and resolving data conflicts using conflict resolution strategies (e.g., last-write-wins, manual conflict resolution) to ensure data consistency and seamless offline user experience.

Chapter 22: Handling Large-scale Data Analytics

Q1: What are the challenges associated with handling large-scale data analytics, and why are they important in system design interviews?

A1: Handling large-scale data analytics presents challenges such as processing massive volumes of data, ensuring timely insights, and managing computational resources efficiently. These challenges are important in system design interviews because they require candidates to demonstrate their understanding of distributed computing, data processing frameworks, and scalability in designing systems for big data analytics.

Q2: What are some common technologies and frameworks used for large-scale data analytics?

A2: Common technologies and frameworks for large-scale data analytics include Apache Hadoop, Apache Spark, Apache Flink, and cloud-based platforms such as Google BigQuery, Amazon Redshift, and Microsoft Azure Data Lake Analytics. These platforms provide capabilities for distributed data processing, parallel computing, and real-time analytics, enabling organizations to derive insights from massive datasets efficiently.

Q3: How do you design a system for large-scale data analytics?

A3: Designing a system for large-scale data analytics involves defining data ingestion pipelines, processing workflows, and analytics engines tailored to specific use cases and requirements. Candidates may discuss architectural patterns such as batch processing, stream processing, and lambda architectures to handle different types of data and processing requirements effectively. They should also consider factors such as data partitioning, fault tolerance, and scalability to design robust and scalable analytics systems.

Q4: What are some optimization techniques for improving the performance of large-scale data analytics systems?

A4: Optimization techniques for improving the performance of large-scale data analytics systems include data partitioning, parallel processing, data compression, and caching. Candidates may discuss strategies such as optimizing data storage formats (e.g., columnar storage), using distributed caching mechanisms (e.g., Redis, Memcached), and employing data pruning and filtering techniques to reduce computational overhead and improve query performance. Additionally, candidates may explore hardware optimizations, such as using high-performance computing (HPC) clusters or specialized hardware accelerators, to further enhance system performance.

Chapter 23: Scalable Infrastructure Design

Q1: What is scalable infrastructure design, and why is it essential in system design interviews?

A1: Scalable infrastructure design involves creating systems that can handle increasing workloads and accommodate growth without sacrificing performance or reliability. It's crucial in system design interviews because it demonstrates a candidate's ability to architect resilient and adaptable systems capable of meeting evolving demands and scaling resources effectively.

Q2: What are some key principles of scalable infrastructure design?

A2: Some key principles of scalable infrastructure design include horizontal scaling, fault tolerance, automation, and elasticity. Horizontal scaling involves adding more resources (e.g., servers, containers) to distribute workload and handle increased traffic. Fault tolerance ensures system resilience by designing for redundancy and failover mechanisms. Automation streamlines deployment, configuration, and management tasks to reduce manual overhead. Elasticity enables systems to dynamically adjust resources based on demand to optimize cost and performance.

Q3: How do you design a scalable infrastructure for web applications?

A3: Designing a scalable infrastructure for web applications involves architecture patterns such as microservices, containerization, and cloud-native technologies. Candidates may discuss strategies such as using auto-scaling groups to add or remove instances based on workload, leveraging container orchestration platforms (e.g., Kubernetes) for managing containerized workloads, and employing cloud services (e.g., AWS, Azure, Google Cloud) for scalable compute, storage, and networking resources.

Q4: What challenges are associated with designing scalable infrastructure, and how can they be addressed?

A4: Challenges associated with designing scalable infrastructure include complexity, cost, and trade-offs between scalability, performance, and reliability. Candidates may discuss solutions such as implementing load balancing to distribute traffic evenly, using distributed caching mechanisms to reduce latency and database load, and adopting event-driven architectures for asynchronous processing and scalability. They should also consider monitoring and optimization techniques to identify bottlenecks, fine-tune resource allocation, and ensure efficient resource utilization as the system scales.

Chapter 24: Designing for IoT (Internet of Things)

Q1: What is the Internet of Things (IoT), and why is designing for IoT important in system design interviews?

A1: The Internet of Things (IoT) refers to the network of interconnected devices embedded with sensors, actuators, and communication capabilities, enabling them to collect and exchange data. Designing for IoT is important in system design interviews because it demonstrates a candidate's understanding of managing heterogeneous devices, handling massive data streams, and ensuring scalability, security, and interoperability in IoT ecosystems.

Q2: What are some key considerations when designing systems for IoT applications?

A2: Key considerations when designing systems for IoT applications include device connectivity, data ingestion, processing, and analysis, security, and device management. Candidates may discuss techniques such as MQTT, CoAP, or HTTP for device communication, edge computing for local data processing, and cloud platforms for scalable data storage and analytics. Additionally, they should address challenges such as device authentication, data encryption, and firmware updates to ensure the security and reliability of IoT systems.

Q3: How do you address scalability challenges in IoT system design?

A3: Addressing scalability challenges in IoT system design involves implementing distributed architectures, edge computing, and scalable cloud infrastructure. Candidates may discuss strategies such as using message brokers for pub/sub communication, deploying edge computing nodes for local data processing and analysis, and leveraging cloud services for scalable storage, compute, and analytics. They should also consider techniques such as data partitioning, sharding, and load balancing to distribute workload and handle increasing numbers of connected devices.

Q4: What are some real-world examples of IoT applications, and how do they illustrate design principles?

A4: Real-world examples of IoT applications include smart homes, industrial automation, healthcare monitoring, and smart cities. These applications illustrate design principles such as sensor integration, data aggregation, real-time analytics, and actionable insights. Candidates may discuss how these applications leverage IoT devices, connectivity protocols, and cloud services to monitor, control, and optimize physical environments, improve operational efficiency, and enhance user experiences.

Chapter 25: Emerging Trends in System Design

Q1: What are some emerging trends in system design, and why are they important in system design interviews?

A1: Emerging trends in system design include serverless computing, edge computing, AI/ML integration, and blockchain technology. These trends are important in system design interviews because they demonstrate candidates' awareness of evolving technologies and their ability to adapt design principles to address new challenges and opportunities in the field of system architecture.

Q2: How does serverless computing impact system design?

A2: Serverless computing abstracts infrastructure management, allowing developers to focus on writing code without worrying about server provisioning or scaling. It enables event-driven architectures, microservices, and cost-effective scaling, but also introduces challenges such as vendor lock-in and cold start latency. Candidates may discuss strategies for optimizing serverless architectures, such as leveraging managed services, designing for scalability, and minimizing function execution times.

Q3: What role does edge computing play in modern system design?

A3: Edge computing brings computing resources closer to the data source, reducing latency and bandwidth usage while enabling real-time processing and decision-making. It is particularly relevant for IoT applications, real-time analytics, and low-latency services. Candidates may discuss edge computing architectures, such as fog computing and decentralized processing, and design considerations such as data locality, security, and orchestration in distributed edge environments.

Q4: How can AI/ML integration impact system design?

A4: AI/ML integration enables intelligent decision-making, predictive analytics, and automation in system design. It is used for tasks such as anomaly detection, recommendation systems, and natural language processing. Candidates may discuss architectural patterns for AI/ML integration, such as model deployment pipelines, feature engineering, and model serving infrastructure. They should also address challenges such as data quality, model explainability, and ethical considerations in AI-driven systems.

Chapter 26: System Design for Cloud Computing

Q1: What is cloud computing, and why is designing for cloud computing important in system design interviews?

A1: Cloud computing refers to the delivery of computing services, including storage, compute power, and databases, over the internet. Designing for cloud computing is crucial in system design interviews because it demonstrates a candidate's understanding of leveraging cloud services, scalability, reliability, and cost optimization in building modern and resilient systems.

Q2: What are some key considerations when designing systems for cloud computing?

A2: Key considerations when designing systems for cloud computing include scalability, elasticity, reliability, security, and cost optimization. Candidates may discuss techniques such as using cloud-native services (e.g., AWS Lambda, Azure Functions), containerization (e.g., Docker, Kubernetes), and serverless architectures to build scalable and resilient systems in the cloud. Additionally, they should address cloud security best practices, compliance requirements, and cost management strategies to optimize resource usage and minimize expenses.

Q3: How do you design for scalability and elasticity in cloud computing?

A3: Designing for scalability and elasticity in cloud computing involves using auto-scaling groups, load balancers, and elastic computing resources to handle varying workloads dynamically. Candidates may discuss strategies such as horizontal scaling, partitioning data, and asynchronous processing to distribute workload across multiple instances or containers and ensure systems can scale up or down based on demand to maintain performance and availability.

Q4: What are some common cloud computing deployment models, and how do they impact system design?

A4: Common cloud computing deployment models include public cloud, private cloud, hybrid cloud, and multi-cloud architectures. Each deployment model has unique characteristics, advantages, and challenges that impact system design. Candidates may discuss considerations such as data residency, compliance requirements, network latency, and vendor lock-in when selecting a deployment model and designing systems for cloud computing. Additionally, they should address strategies for workload distribution, data replication, and disaster recovery across different cloud environments to ensure resilience and business continuity.

Chapter 27: Designing for Real-Time Communication Systems

Q1: What are the key components to consider when designing real-time communication systems?

A1: When designing real-time communication systems, key components to consider include messaging protocols, signaling mechanisms, media codecs, network infrastructure, and user interface design. These components collectively enable seamless and low-latency communication experiences across different devices and platforms.

Q2: How do you ensure scalability and reliability in real-time communication systems?

A2: Ensuring scalability and reliability in real-time communication systems involves designing for distributed architectures, redundancy, fault tolerance, and load balancing. Candidates may discuss techniques such as using message brokers for pub/sub communication, deploying redundant signaling servers, and leveraging cloud-based infrastructure for horizontal scaling and high availability.

Q3: What role does WebRTC (Web Real-Time Communication) play in designing real-time communication systems?

A3: WebRTC is a standardized framework for enabling real-time communication capabilities directly in web browsers and mobile applications. It provides APIs for audio/video communication, data sharing, and peer-to-peer networking, allowing developers to build seamless and interoperable communication experiences without the need for plugins or third-party software.

Q4: What are some challenges associated with designing real-time communication systems, and how can they be addressed?

A4: Challenges associated with designing real-time communication systems include network congestion, latency, jitter, packet loss, and device compatibility. Candidates may discuss strategies such as implementing adaptive bitrate streaming, using error correction techniques, optimizing media codecs for low-latency transmission, and prioritizing traffic based on quality of service (QoS) metrics to address these challenges and ensure a smooth user experience.

Chapter 28: System Design for Video Streaming Platforms

Q1: What are the key components to consider when designing video streaming platforms?

A1: When designing video streaming platforms, key components to consider include content ingestion, transcoding, storage, content delivery network (CDN), playback clients, and analytics. These components work together to deliver high-quality video content to users across various devices and network conditions.

Q2: How do you ensure scalability and reliability in video streaming platforms?

A2: Ensuring scalability and reliability in video streaming platforms involves designing for distributed architectures, redundancy, and load balancing. Candidates may discuss techniques such as using cloud-based infrastructure for horizontal scaling, deploying redundant transcoding and storage servers, and leveraging CDN for efficient content delivery to global audiences.

Q3: What are some challenges associated with designing video streaming platforms, and how can they be addressed?

A3: Challenges associated with designing video streaming platforms include bandwidth constraints, latency, video quality, and content protection. Candidates may discuss strategies such as implementing adaptive bitrate streaming, optimizing video codecs for efficient compression, using content encryption and digital rights management (DRM) solutions to protect intellectual property, and deploying edge caching to reduce latency and improve user experience.

Q4: How do you optimize video streaming platforms for different devices and network conditions?

A4: Optimizing video streaming platforms for different devices and network conditions involves adaptive streaming techniques, device detection, and network optimization. Candidates may discuss approaches such as dynamic bitrate adaptation, responsive video players, content preloading, and CDN selection based on user location and network performance metrics to ensure smooth playback and minimize buffering across diverse devices and network environments.

Chapter 29: Designing Highly Available Data Storage Systems

Q1: What are the key considerations when designing highly available data storage systems?

A1: When designing highly available data storage systems, key considerations include redundancy, fault tolerance, data replication, consistency models, and scalability. These factors ensure that data is accessible, reliable, and consistent even in the event of hardware failures or network partitions.

Q2: How do you ensure data integrity and consistency in highly available data storage systems?

A2: Ensuring data integrity and consistency in highly available data storage systems involves implementing replication mechanisms, distributed transactions, and consistency protocols. Candidates may discuss techniques such as quorum-based replication, two-phase commit, and eventual consistency to maintain data integrity and consistency guarantees across distributed storage nodes.

Q3: What strategies can be employed to achieve fault tolerance in data storage systems?

A3: Achieving fault tolerance in data storage systems involves designing for redundancy, failover mechanisms, and data recovery strategies. Candidates may discuss techniques such as data mirroring, RAID configurations, hot standby servers, and automatic failover mechanisms to minimize downtime and ensure continuous data availability in the event of hardware failures or system crashes.

Q4: How do you design scalable data storage systems to handle growing volumes of data?

A4: Designing scalable data storage systems involves using distributed architectures, partitioning strategies, and horizontal scaling techniques. Candidates may discuss approaches such as sharding, consistent hashing, and data partitioning based on key ranges or hash values to distribute data across multiple storage nodes and accommodate increasing data volumes while maintaining performance and availability.

Chapter 30: Scalable Search Engine Design

Q1: What are the key components to consider when designing a scalable search engine?

A1: When designing a scalable search engine, key components to consider include indexing, query processing, ranking algorithms, distributed storage, and retrieval mechanisms. These components work together to efficiently index, store, and retrieve relevant information from a large corpus of data.

Q2: How do you ensure scalability and performance in a search engine design?

A2: Ensuring scalability and performance in a search engine design involves distributed architectures, sharding, caching, and parallel processing. Candidates may discuss techniques such as horizontal scaling across multiple servers, partitioning indexes into shards, caching frequently accessed documents or query results, and parallelizing query processing to handle increasing query loads efficiently.

Q3: What are some challenges associated with designing scalable search engines, and how can they be addressed?

A3: Challenges associated with designing scalable search engines include index partitioning, query routing, relevance ranking, and real-time indexing. Candidates may discuss strategies such as consistent hashing for index partitioning, query routing based on distributed routing tables or load balancers, relevance ranking algorithms such as TF-IDF or BM25, and incremental indexing techniques to handle continuous updates and changes in the data corpus.

Q4: How do you optimize search engine design for different types of queries and user interactions?

A4: Optimizing search engine design for different types of queries and user interactions involves query analysis, query rewriting, and result presentation. Candidates may discuss techniques such as query expansion, spell correction, synonym detection, and faceted search to enhance query understanding and improve search accuracy. They should also address strategies for presenting search results, such as snippet generation, result clustering, and personalized ranking, to provide relevant and actionable information to users.

Chapter 31: System Design for Social Networking Platforms

Q1: What are the key components to consider when designing a system for social networking platforms?

A1: When designing a system for social networking platforms, key components include user profiles, friend relationships, content creation and sharing, newsfeeds, messaging systems, notifications, and privacy controls. These components collectively enable users to connect, interact, and share content within the social network.

Q2: How do you ensure scalability and performance in a social networking platform design?

A2: Ensuring scalability and performance in a social networking platform design involves distributed architectures, caching, asynchronous processing, and load balancing. Candidates may discuss techniques such as sharding user data, caching frequently accessed content or user profiles, and using message queues for asynchronous processing of background tasks such as notifications and feed updates to handle increasing user activity and content volume.

Q3: What are some challenges associated with designing social networking platforms, and how can they be addressed?

A3: Challenges associated with designing social networking platforms include scalability, privacy concerns, spam prevention, and content moderation. Candidates may discuss strategies such as implementing rate limiting and anti-spam filters to prevent abuse, using machine learning algorithms for content moderation and sentiment analysis, and providing granular privacy controls and user permissions to empower users to manage their data and interactions effectively.

Q4: How do you design personalized user experiences in social networking platforms?

A4: Designing personalized user experiences in social networking platforms involves user profiling, recommendation systems, and personalization algorithms. Candidates may discuss techniques such as collaborative filtering, content-based filtering, and hybrid recommendation approaches to analyze user preferences, interests, and behavior and recommend relevant content, connections, or groups tailored to individual users' interests and activities within the social network.

Chapter 32: Building Scalable Logging and Monitoring Systems

Q1: What are the key components to consider when building a scalable logging and monitoring system?

A1: When building a scalable logging and monitoring system, key components include log aggregation, storage, indexing, search, visualization, alerting, and distributed data collection agents. These components work together to collect, store, analyze, and visualize log data from distributed systems and applications.

Q2: How do you ensure scalability and performance in a logging and monitoring system design?

A2: Ensuring scalability and performance in a logging and monitoring system design involves distributed architectures, partitioning, data sharding, and efficient data processing. Candidates may discuss techniques such as using distributed data stores (e.g., Elasticsearch, Apache Kafka) for log storage and indexing, employing stream processing frameworks (e.g., Apache Flink, Apache Spark) for real-time data analysis, and horizontal scaling of monitoring agents and data collectors to handle increasing data volumes and processing requirements.

Q3: What are some challenges associated with building scalable logging and monitoring systems, and how can they be addressed?

A3: Challenges associated with building scalable logging and monitoring systems include data volume, data retention, real-time processing, and alerting. Candidates may discuss strategies such as data sampling, log rotation, and log aggregation to manage data volume and retention, implementing stream processing pipelines for real-time data analysis and anomaly detection, and setting up alerting mechanisms based on predefined thresholds or machine learning models to notify operators of potential issues or incidents.

Q4: How do you design for fault tolerance and reliability in logging and monitoring systems?

A4: Designing for fault tolerance and reliability in logging and monitoring systems involves redundancy, failover mechanisms, and data replication. Candidates may discuss techniques such as deploying redundant data collectors and monitoring agents across multiple nodes or regions, using distributed consensus protocols (e.g., Apache ZooKeeper, etcd) for leader election and coordination, and replicating critical monitoring data and metadata across multiple storage nodes to ensure data durability and availability in the event of node failures or network partitions.

Chapter 33: Designing for High Throughput Messaging Systems

Q1: What are the key components to consider when designing a high throughput messaging system?

A1: When designing a high throughput messaging system, key components include message brokers, producers, consumers, topics or queues, message serialization formats, and delivery guarantees. These components work together to enable the reliable and efficient exchange of messages between distributed systems and applications.

Q2: How do you ensure scalability and performance in a high throughput messaging system design?

A2: Ensuring scalability and performance in a high throughput messaging system design involves distributed architectures, partitioning, and parallel processing. Candidates may discuss techniques such as using partitioned message queues, employing message brokers with horizontal scaling capabilities (e.g., Apache Kafka, RabbitMQ), and optimizing message serialization and compression to reduce network overhead and latency and handle increasing message volumes efficiently.

Q3: What are some challenges associated with designing high throughput messaging systems, and how can they be addressed?

A3: Challenges associated with designing high throughput messaging systems include message ordering, message loss, and message duplication. Candidates may discuss strategies such as implementing message acknowledgments and delivery guarantees (e.g., at-least-once, exactly-once), using sequence numbers or timestamps for message ordering, and implementing idempotent message processing to handle duplicate messages and ensure data consistency and correctness.

Q4: How do you design for fault tolerance and reliability in high throughput messaging systems?

A4: Designing for fault tolerance and reliability in high throughput messaging systems involves redundancy, replication, and failover mechanisms. Candidates may discuss techniques such as deploying redundant message brokers with data replication across multiple nodes or data centers, using distributed consensus protocols (e.g., Apache ZooKeeper) for leader election and coordination, and implementing message acknowledgments and retry mechanisms to handle message delivery failures and ensure message durability and reliability.

Chapter 34: Implementing Data Warehousing Solutions

Q1: What are the key components to consider when implementing a data warehousing solution?

A1: When implementing a data warehousing solution, key components include data sources, ETL (Extract, Transform, Load) processes, data storage, data modeling, query processing, and reporting or analytics tools. These components work together to aggregate, clean, store, and analyze large volumes of data from disparate sources for business intelligence and decision-making purposes.

Q2: How do you ensure scalability and performance in a data warehousing solution design?

A2: Ensuring scalability and performance in a data warehousing solution design involves optimizing data processing pipelines, data storage, and query performance. Candidates may discuss techniques such as parallel processing, partitioning, and indexing to optimize ETL processes and data retrieval, using distributed storage systems (e.g., Hadoop Distributed File System, Amazon Redshift) for scalable data storage, and employing query optimization techniques (e.g., query rewriting, query caching) to improve query performance and response times.

Q3: What are some challenges associated with implementing data warehousing solutions, and how can they be addressed?

A3: Challenges associated with implementing data warehousing solutions include data quality, data integration, schema evolution, and data governance. Candidates may discuss strategies such as data profiling and cleansing to ensure data quality, implementing data integration tools (e.g., Apache NiFi, Talend) for seamless data ingestion and transformation, and using schema evolution techniques (e.g., versioning, backward compatibility) to accommodate changes in data structures and requirements. Additionally, establishing data governance policies and practices (e.g., data lineage tracking, access controls) can help ensure data integrity, security, and compliance with regulatory requirements.

Q4: How do you design for fault tolerance and reliability in data warehousing solutions?

A4: Designing for fault tolerance and reliability in data warehousing solutions involves redundancy, data backup, and disaster recovery planning. Candidates may discuss techniques such as data replication across multiple storage nodes or data centers, implementing automated backup and restore processes, and setting up disaster recovery sites or failover mechanisms to ensure continuous data availability and minimize downtime in the event of hardware failures, data corruption, or natural disasters.

Chapter 35: Designing Scalable Machine Learning Pipelines

Q1: What are the key components to consider when designing scalable machine learning pipelines?

A1: When designing scalable machine learning pipelines, key components include data ingestion, preprocessing, model training, evaluation, deployment, and monitoring. These components work together to automate the end-to-end process of building, training, and deploying machine learning models at scale.

Q2: How do you ensure scalability and performance in a machine learning pipeline design?

A2: Ensuring scalability and performance in a machine learning pipeline design involves distributed processing, parallelization, and optimization of computational resources. Candidates may discuss techniques such as using distributed computing frameworks (e.g., Apache Spark, TensorFlow), data partitioning, and model parallelization to distribute workloads across multiple nodes or GPUs and leverage hardware accelerators for faster model training and inference.

Q3: What are some challenges associated with designing scalable machine learning pipelines, and how can they be addressed?

A3: Challenges associated with designing scalable machine learning pipelines include data variety, data quality, model complexity, and deployment latency. Candidates may discuss strategies such as data preprocessing and feature engineering to handle diverse data types and improve model performance, implementing model versioning and experimentation frameworks for managing model complexity and reproducibility, and using containerization and serverless architectures for efficient model deployment and scaling.

Q4: How do you design for fault tolerance and reliability in machine learning pipelines?

A4: Designing for fault tolerance and reliability in machine learning pipelines involves error handling, model versioning, and automated monitoring. Candidates may discuss techniques such as implementing retry mechanisms and error logging to handle transient failures and recover from system errors, maintaining version control for models, data, and code to ensure reproducibility and rollback capabilities, and setting up automated monitoring and alerting systems to detect anomalies and performance degradation in real-time for proactive intervention.

Chapter 36: System Design for Collaborative Editing Platforms

Q1: What are the key components to consider when designing a system for collaborative editing platforms?

A1: When designing a system for collaborative editing platforms, key components include real-time synchronization, conflict resolution, user authentication, access control, versioning, and messaging infrastructure. These components work together to enable multiple users to edit shared documents concurrently while maintaining data consistency and integrity.

Q2: How do you ensure scalability and performance in a collaborative editing platform design?

A2: Ensuring scalability and performance in a collaborative editing platform design involves distributed architectures, operational transformation (OT) algorithms, and efficient data synchronization mechanisms. Candidates may discuss techniques such as using distributed databases or key-value stores for storing collaborative documents, implementing server-side and client-side caching to reduce latency, and optimizing network protocols (e.g., WebSockets) for real-time communication and data synchronization.

Q3: What are some challenges associated with designing collaborative editing platforms, and how can they be addressed?

A3: Challenges associated with designing collaborative editing platforms include conflict resolution, offline editing, and user awareness. Candidates may discuss strategies such as operational transformation (OT) or conflict-free replicated data types (CRDTs) for resolving concurrent edits and merge conflicts, implementing offline-first architectures and conflict resolution policies to handle intermittent network connectivity, and providing user feedback and presence indicators to enhance user awareness and collaboration experience.

Q4: How do you design for fault tolerance and reliability in collaborative editing platforms?

A4: Designing for fault tolerance and reliability in collaborative editing platforms involves replication, consistency guarantees, and fault recovery mechanisms. Candidates may discuss techniques such as replicating document state across multiple servers or data centers to ensure availability and durability, using consensus algorithms (e.g., Paxos, Raft) for achieving strong consistency guarantees, and implementing automatic conflict resolution and version control mechanisms to recover from failures and maintain data integrity in the face of network partitions or server crashes.

Chapter 37: Designing Geographic Information Systems (GIS)

Q1: What are the key components to consider when designing a Geographic Information System (GIS)?

A1: When designing a GIS, key components include spatial data storage, data acquisition, data processing, geospatial analysis, visualization, and user interfaces. These components work together to capture, store, analyze, and present geographic data and information.

Q2: How do you ensure scalability and performance in a GIS design?

A2: Ensuring scalability and performance in a GIS design involves optimizing spatial indexing, data partitioning, and distributed processing. Candidates may discuss techniques such as using spatial indexing structures (e.g., R-trees, Quad-trees) for efficient spatial data retrieval, partitioning spatial datasets across multiple nodes or shards, and leveraging parallel processing frameworks (e.g., Apache Spark, Hadoop) for distributed geospatial analysis and computation.

Q3: What are some challenges associated with designing Geographic Information Systems, and how can they be addressed?

A3: Challenges associated with designing Geographic Information Systems include data heterogeneity, data interoperability, and spatial data processing complexity. Candidates may discuss strategies such as data standardization and normalization to address data heterogeneity, implementing data integration and interoperability standards (e.g., OGC standards) for seamless data exchange between different GIS platforms, and using spatial analysis libraries and tools (e.g., PostGIS, GeoPandas) for complex geospatial analysis and modeling.

Q4: How do you design for fault tolerance and reliability in Geographic Information Systems?

A4: Designing for fault tolerance and reliability in Geographic Information Systems involves data replication, disaster recovery, and fault-tolerant architectures. Candidates may discuss techniques such as replicating spatial datasets across multiple storage nodes or data centers to ensure data availability and durability, setting up backup and recovery processes for disaster recovery, and deploying redundant server clusters and load balancers to handle high availability and fault tolerance requirements.

Chapter 38: Building Resilient Microservices Architectures

Q1: What are the key considerations when building resilient microservices architectures?

A1: When building resilient microservices architectures, key considerations include fault isolation, service discovery, load balancing, circuit breaking, and distributed tracing. These considerations ensure that microservices can tolerate failures, maintain availability, and provide consistent performance in distributed environments.

Q2: How do you ensure fault tolerance in a microservices architecture?

A2: Ensuring fault tolerance in a microservices architecture involves implementing redundancy, graceful degradation, and failure recovery mechanisms. Candidates may discuss techniques such as deploying microservices in containerized environments (e.g., Docker, Kubernetes) for isolation and scalability, using service meshes (e.g., Istio, Linkerd) for service discovery and traffic management, and implementing retry and fallback strategies to handle transient failures and degraded service conditions.

Q3: What are some challenges associated with building resilient microservices architectures, and how can they be addressed?

A3: Challenges associated with building resilient microservices architectures include distributed data consistency, service coordination, and network latency. Candidates may discuss strategies such as implementing eventual consistency models for distributed data stores, using distributed transactions or compensating transactions for coordinating updates across multiple services, and optimizing network communication (e.g., reducing chattiness, implementing caching) to minimize latency and improve system performance and reliability.

Q4: How do you design for scalability and elasticity in microservices architectures?

A4: Designing for scalability and elasticity in microservices architectures involves service decomposition, statelessness, and horizontal scaling. Candidates may discuss techniques such as breaking down monolithic applications into smaller, loosely coupled microservices, designing stateless microservices that can be scaled independently, and using container orchestration platforms (e.g., Kubernetes, Amazon ECS) for dynamic scaling based on workload demand to achieve high availability and efficient resource utilization.

Chapter 39: System Design for Online Marketplaces

Q1: What are the key components to consider when designing a system for online marketplaces?

A1: When designing a system for online marketplaces, key components include user accounts, product listings, search and recommendation engines, shopping carts, payment gateways, order management, and seller management tools. These components work together to facilitate seamless transactions between buyers and sellers in a digital marketplace environment.

Q2: How do you ensure scalability and performance in a system for online marketplaces?

A2: Ensuring scalability and performance in a system for online marketplaces involves distributed architectures, caching, and load balancing. Candidates may discuss techniques such as using distributed databases or sharded databases for storing product and transaction data, employing content delivery networks (CDNs) for efficient content delivery, and implementing horizontal scaling and auto-scaling mechanisms to handle increasing user traffic and transaction volumes.

Q3: What are some challenges associated with designing systems for online marketplaces, and how can they be addressed?

A3: Challenges associated with designing systems for online marketplaces include inventory management, fraud prevention, and user trust and safety. Candidates may discuss strategies such as implementing inventory tracking and synchronization mechanisms to manage product availability across multiple sellers, using fraud detection algorithms and identity verification processes to mitigate fraudulent activities, and providing robust user feedback and dispute resolution mechanisms to foster trust and safety within the marketplace community.

Q4: How do you design for fault tolerance and reliability in systems for online marketplaces?

A4: Designing for fault tolerance and reliability in systems for online marketplaces involves redundancy, data replication, and disaster recovery planning. Candidates may discuss techniques such as deploying redundant server clusters and load balancers to ensure high availability of marketplace services, replicating critical data (e.g., user profiles, transaction logs) across multiple data centers or cloud regions for data durability and fault tolerance, and setting up backup and recovery processes for disaster recovery in the event of system failures or outages.

Chapter 40: Designing High-Performance Database Systems

Q1: What are the key factors to consider when designing high-performance database systems?

A1: When designing high-performance database systems, key factors include database schema design, indexing strategies, query optimization, data partitioning, caching mechanisms, and hardware infrastructure. These factors collectively contribute to optimizing data retrieval, storage, and processing to achieve superior database performance.

Q2: How do you ensure scalability in a high-performance database system?

A2: Ensuring scalability in a high-performance database system involves employing distributed architectures, horizontal scaling techniques, and partitioning strategies. Candidates may discuss approaches such as sharding the database across multiple servers, using distributed databases or NoSQL solutions, and implementing data partitioning based on key ranges or hash values to distribute data and queries across multiple nodes and handle increasing data volumes and query loads.

Q3: What are some challenges associated with designing high-performance database systems, and how can they be addressed?

A3: Challenges associated with designing high-performance database systems include concurrency control, data consistency, and resource contention. Candidates may discuss strategies such as implementing multi-version concurrency control (MVCC) or optimistic concurrency control (OCC) mechanisms to manage concurrent transactions and avoid deadlock or contention, using distributed locking and isolation protocols to ensure data consistency and integrity in distributed environments, and optimizing resource utilization (e.g., memory, CPU) through query optimization, indexing, and caching to improve database performance and throughput.

Q4: How do you design for fault tolerance and reliability in high-performance database systems?

A4: Designing for fault tolerance and reliability in high-performance database systems involves data replication, failover mechanisms, and disaster recovery planning. Candidates may discuss techniques such as deploying database replication across multiple nodes or data centers to ensure data availability and durability, setting up automatic failover and recovery processes to handle node failures or network partitions, and implementing backup and restore procedures for data recovery in the event of catastrophic failures or data corruption.

Chapter 41: Building Real-Time Analytics Platforms

Q1: What are the key components to consider when building a real-time analytics platform?

A1: When building a real-time analytics platform, key components include data ingestion, stream processing, storage, analytics engines, visualization tools, and alerting mechanisms. These components work together to enable organizations to collect, process, analyze, and visualize streaming data in real-time to gain actionable insights and make informed decisions.

Q2: How do you ensure scalability and performance in a real-time analytics platform design?

A2: Ensuring scalability and performance in a real-time analytics platform design involves distributed architectures, parallel processing, and optimization of data pipelines. Candidates may discuss techniques such as using distributed stream processing frameworks (e.g., Apache Kafka, Apache Flink) for handling high throughput and low latency data streams, employing horizontal scaling and auto-scaling mechanisms to dynamically allocate computational resources based on workload demands, and optimizing data ingestion and processing pipelines for efficient resource utilization and minimal processing latency.

Q3: What are some challenges associated with building real-time analytics platforms, and how can they be addressed?

A3: Challenges associated with building real-time analytics platforms include data consistency, data quality, and processing latency. Candidates may discuss strategies such as implementing event time processing and windowing techniques to handle out-of-order events and ensure data consistency across distributed streams, using data validation and cleansing processes to improve data quality and accuracy, and optimizing data processing algorithms and infrastructure to minimize processing latency and ensure timely delivery of insights and alerts to end-users.

Q4: How do you design for fault tolerance and reliability in real-time analytics platforms?

A4: Designing for fault tolerance and reliability in real-time analytics platforms involves redundancy, data replication, and fault recovery mechanisms. Candidates may discuss techniques such as deploying distributed data stores (e.g., Apache Cassandra, Amazon DynamoDB) with built-in replication and fault tolerance features to ensure data availability and durability, setting up data backup and disaster recovery processes to recover from hardware failures or data corruption, and implementing checkpointing and stateful stream processing to maintain processing state and ensure fault recovery in the event of node failures or system crashes.

Chapter 42: Designing for Multi-Region Disaster Recovery

Q1: What factors should be considered when designing a multi-region disaster recovery system?

A1: When designing a multi-region disaster recovery system, factors such as geographic diversity, data replication, latency, failover mechanisms, and data consistency need to be carefully considered. These factors ensure that the system can withstand regional outages and maintain data integrity and availability during disaster scenarios.

Q2: How do you ensure data consistency in a multi-region disaster recovery setup?

A2: Ensuring data consistency in a multi-region disaster recovery setup involves implementing synchronous or asynchronous replication mechanisms, consistency models, and conflict resolution strategies. Candidates may discuss techniques such as multi-master replication with distributed consensus protocols (e.g., Paxos, Raft), eventual consistency with conflict resolution mechanisms (e.g., vector clocks, last-write-wins), and transaction coordination across distributed databases to maintain data consistency across multiple regions.

Q3: What are some challenges associated with designing multi-region disaster recovery systems, and how can they be addressed?

A3: Challenges associated with designing multi-region disaster recovery systems include network latency, data transfer costs, and failover complexity. Candidates may discuss strategies such as using content delivery networks (CDNs) or dedicated inter-region links to minimize network latency and improve data transfer speeds, optimizing data replication and synchronization processes to reduce data transfer costs, and implementing automated failover orchestration and testing procedures to streamline failover operations and ensure system reliability and readiness during disaster events.

Q4: How do you validate the effectiveness of a multi-region disaster recovery setup?

A4: Validating the effectiveness of a multi-region disaster recovery setup involves conducting regular disaster recovery drills, failover tests, and performance monitoring. Candidates may discuss techniques such as simulating regional outages or infrastructure failures to test failover mechanisms and data recovery procedures, measuring key performance metrics (e.g., recovery time objective, recovery point objective) to assess system readiness and resilience, and using monitoring and alerting systems to detect and respond to potential issues or anomalies in real-time, ensuring continuous monitoring and improvement of the disaster recovery setup.

Chapter 43: System Design for Gaming Platforms

Q1: What are the essential components to consider when designing a system for gaming platforms?

A1: When designing a system for gaming platforms, essential components include user authentication, game state management, matchmaking, real-time communication, leaderboard tracking, and payment processing. These components work together to create an immersive gaming experience while ensuring security, fairness, and scalability.

Q2: How do you ensure scalability and performance in a gaming platform design?

A2: Ensuring scalability and performance in a gaming platform design involves distributed architectures, caching, and load balancing. Candidates may discuss techniques such as using microservices or serverless architectures for scalability, implementing content delivery networks (CDNs) for efficient content delivery, and optimizing network protocols for real-time communication to minimize latency and improve responsiveness.

Q3: What are some challenges associated with designing systems for gaming platforms, and how can they be addressed?

A3: Challenges associated with designing systems for gaming platforms include network latency, cheating prevention, and data consistency. Candidates may discuss strategies such as implementing predictive latency compensation techniques to mitigate network latency effects, using anti-cheat mechanisms and server-side validation to prevent cheating and maintain game integrity, and employing distributed databases or replication mechanisms to ensure data consistency across game servers and regions.

Q4: How do you design for fault tolerance and reliability in gaming platforms?

A4: Designing for fault tolerance and reliability in gaming platforms involves redundancy, failover mechanisms, and disaster recovery planning. Candidates may discuss techniques such as deploying redundant game servers and load balancers to handle traffic spikes and ensure high availability, setting up automatic failover and recovery processes to handle server failures or network disruptions, and implementing backup and restore procedures for disaster recovery in the event of data loss or corruption.

Chapter 44: Building Scalable ETL (Extract, Transform, Load) Pipelines

Q1: What are the key components involved in building scalable ETL pipelines?

A1: Building scalable ETL pipelines involves several key components, including data extraction sources, transformation processes, data loading destinations, scheduling mechanisms, error handling, and monitoring systems. These components work together to efficiently extract, transform, and load data from various sources into a target system.

Q2: How do you ensure scalability in ETL pipeline design?

A2: Ensuring scalability in ETL pipeline design involves partitioning data processing tasks, parallelizing data transformations, and utilizing distributed processing frameworks. Candidates may discuss techniques such as partitioning data across multiple nodes or shards, leveraging distributed computing frameworks like Apache Spark or Apache Flink for parallel processing, and using queue-based or event-driven architectures to scale data ingestion and processing horizontally.

Q3: What are some challenges associated with building scalable ETL pipelines, and how can they be addressed?

A3: Challenges associated with building scalable ETL pipelines include data consistency, schema evolution, and dependency management. Candidates may discuss strategies such as implementing transactional processing and checkpointing mechanisms to ensure data consistency during ETL operations, adopting schema-on-read approaches or schema evolution techniques to accommodate changes in data formats or structures, and using dependency management tools or workflow orchestration platforms to manage complex data transformation workflows and dependencies.

Q4: How do you design for fault tolerance and reliability in ETL pipelines?

A4: Designing for fault tolerance and reliability in ETL pipelines involves implementing error handling mechanisms, retry strategies, and data recovery processes. Candidates may discuss techniques such as using idempotent operations and transactional processing for data consistency and error recovery, implementing retry and backoff strategies for handling transient failures or network issues, and setting up monitoring and alerting systems to detect data processing errors or pipeline failures in real-time for timely intervention and resolution.

Chapter 45: Designing for Internet-Scale Messaging Systems

Q1: What are the fundamental components in designing internet-scale messaging systems?

A1: Designing internet-scale messaging systems involves several fundamental components, including message brokers, message queues, publishers, subscribers, routing mechanisms, and scalability features. These components facilitate the reliable and efficient exchange of messages across distributed systems at internet scale.

Q2: How can you ensure scalability in internet-scale messaging system design?

A2: Ensuring scalability in internet-scale messaging system design involves deploying distributed architectures, partitioning message queues, and employing horizontal scaling techniques. Candidates may discuss approaches such as using partitioned message brokers or distributed message queues to handle increased message volumes, implementing sharding or partitioning strategies to distribute message processing across multiple nodes, and utilizing load balancing and auto-scaling mechanisms to dynamically adjust resources based on workload demands.

Q3: What challenges might arise when designing internet-scale messaging systems, and how can they be addressed?

A3: Challenges associated with designing internet-scale messaging systems include message ordering, delivery guarantees, and network latency. Candidates may discuss strategies such as implementing message sequencing mechanisms or using event sourcing patterns to maintain message ordering guarantees, employing acknowledgment and retry mechanisms for ensuring message delivery guarantees, and optimizing network protocols and routing algorithms to minimize latency and improve message throughput and responsiveness.

Q4: How do you design for fault tolerance and reliability in internet-scale messaging systems?

A4: Designing for fault tolerance and reliability in internet-scale messaging systems involves redundancy, data replication, and failover mechanisms. Candidates may discuss techniques such as deploying replicated message brokers or distributed message queues across multiple data centers or cloud regions to ensure high availability and data durability, implementing message acknowledgments and persistent message storage for fault-tolerant message delivery, and setting up automatic failover and recovery processes to handle node failures or network partitions and maintain uninterrupted message processing and delivery.

Chapter 46: System Design for Healthcare Information Systems

Q1: What are the critical considerations in designing healthcare information systems?

A1: Designing healthcare information systems requires careful consideration of patient data privacy, regulatory compliance, interoperability standards, data security, and system scalability. These considerations ensure the system effectively manages sensitive healthcare information while complying with industry regulations and facilitating seamless data exchange between healthcare providers.

Q2: How do you ensure data security and patient privacy in healthcare information system design?

A2: Ensuring data security and patient privacy in healthcare information system design involves implementing encryption techniques, access controls, audit trails, and secure authentication mechanisms. Candidates may discuss strategies such as encrypting sensitive data at rest and in transit, enforcing role-based access controls to restrict data access based on user roles and permissions, maintaining detailed audit logs for tracking data access and modifications, and implementing two-factor authentication or biometric authentication for user identity verification.

Q3: What challenges might arise when designing healthcare information systems, and how can they be addressed?

A3: Challenges associated with designing healthcare information systems include data standardization, data integration, and system interoperability. Candidates may discuss solutions such as adopting interoperability standards (e.g., HL7, FHIR) for seamless data exchange between different healthcare systems and applications, implementing data normalization and mapping techniques to integrate disparate healthcare datasets, and leveraging healthcare information exchange (HIE) networks or APIs for facilitating secure data sharing and collaboration among healthcare providers.

Q4: How do you design for fault tolerance and reliability in healthcare information systems?

A4: Designing for fault tolerance and reliability in healthcare information systems involves redundancy, disaster recovery planning, and data backup mechanisms. Candidates may discuss techniques such as deploying redundant server clusters and load balancers to ensure high availability of healthcare services, setting up data replication and backup processes across multiple data centers or cloud regions for data durability and disaster recovery, and implementing automated failover and recovery procedures to minimize downtime and ensure uninterrupted access to critical healthcare information and services.

Chapter 47: Building Scalable Event-Driven Architectures

Q1: What are the key components in building scalable event-driven architectures?

A1: Building scalable event-driven architectures involves several key components, including event producers, event brokers, event processors, event consumers, and scalability features such as partitioning, sharding, and distributed processing. These components facilitate the seamless processing and propagation of events across distributed systems while ensuring scalability and reliability.

Q2: How do you ensure scalability in event-driven architecture design?

A2: Ensuring scalability in event-driven architecture design involves employing distributed architectures, message partitioning, and horizontal scaling techniques. Candidates may discuss approaches such as using distributed message brokers or event streaming platforms for handling high throughput and low latency event streams, implementing message partitioning or sharding strategies to distribute event processing across multiple nodes, and leveraging containerization or serverless computing for dynamic resource allocation and scaling based on workload demands.

Q3: What challenges might arise when building scalable event-driven architectures, and how can they be addressed?

A3: Challenges associated with building scalable event-driven architectures include event ordering, data consistency, and fault tolerance. Candidates may discuss strategies such as implementing event sequencing mechanisms or using event sourcing patterns to maintain event ordering guarantees, employing distributed transaction protocols or compensating transaction patterns to ensure data consistency across distributed systems, and designing fault-tolerant architectures with redundancy, replication, and automated failover mechanisms to handle node failures or network partitions and ensure continuous event processing and delivery.

Q4: How do you design for fault tolerance and reliability in event-driven architectures?

A4: Designing for fault tolerance and reliability in event-driven architectures involves redundancy, data replication, and failover mechanisms. Candidates may discuss techniques such as deploying replicated event brokers or distributed message queues across multiple data centers or cloud regions to ensure high availability and data durability, implementing acknowledgment and retry mechanisms for fault-tolerant event delivery, and setting up automatic failover and recovery processes to handle node failures or network disruptions and maintain uninterrupted event processing and propagation across distributed systems.

Chapter 48: Designing Distributed File Systems

Q1: What are the essential components to consider when designing distributed file systems?

A1: Designing distributed file systems involves several essential components, including metadata servers, data storage nodes, file access protocols, replication mechanisms, consistency models, and fault tolerance features. These components work together to enable distributed storage, access, and management of files across multiple nodes in a network.

Q2: How do you ensure scalability in distributed file system design?

A2: Ensuring scalability in distributed file system design involves partitioning data, parallelizing access, and employing distributed storage architectures. Candidates may discuss techniques such as sharding or partitioning data across multiple storage nodes to distribute data and access load, implementing distributed file system protocols (e.g., HDFS, NFSv4) for parallel file access and data retrieval, and using horizontal scaling and auto-scaling mechanisms to dynamically allocate storage resources based on workload demands.

Q3: What challenges might arise when designing distributed file systems, and how can they be addressed?

A3: Challenges
associated with designing distributed file systems include data consistency, metadata management, and network latency. Candidates may discuss strategies such as implementing distributed locking or consensus protocols for maintaining data consistency and preventing concurrent modifications, using distributed metadata management systems (e.g., ZooKeeper, etcd) for centralized metadata coordination and synchronization, and optimizing network protocols and data transfer mechanisms to minimize latency and improve file access and retrieval performance in distributed environments.

Q4: How do you design for fault tolerance and reliability in distributed file systems?

A4: Designing for fault tolerance and reliability in distributed file systems involves redundancy, data replication, and error recovery mechanisms. Candidates may discuss techniques such as deploying redundant storage nodes and metadata servers to ensure high availability and data durability, setting up data replication and synchronization processes to maintain multiple copies of data across distributed nodes or data centers for fault tolerance, and implementing error detection and recovery mechanisms (e.g., checksums, error correction codes) to detect and correct data corruption or loss in distributed file systems.

Chapter 49: System Design for IoT (Internet of Things) Platforms

Q1: What are the fundamental components to consider when designing a system for IoT platforms?

A1: Designing a system for IoT platforms involves key components such as IoT devices, edge computing nodes, connectivity protocols, data ingestion mechanisms, data processing engines, and analytics platforms. These components enable the collection, processing, and analysis of sensor data from connected devices to derive actionable insights and facilitate automation.

Q2: How do you ensure scalability and performance in IoT platform design?

A2: Ensuring scalability and performance in IoT platform design involves leveraging distributed architectures, edge computing, and efficient data processing techniques. Candidates may discuss approaches such as deploying edge computing nodes to perform data preprocessing and filtering close to the data source, using message queuing or streaming platforms for scalable and real-time data ingestion, and employing distributed data processing frameworks like Apache Spark or Apache Flink for analyzing large volumes of IoT data in parallel.

Q3: What challenges might arise when designing systems for IoT platforms, and how can they be addressed?

A3: Challenges associated with designing systems for IoT platforms include data security, interoperability, and device management. Candidates may discuss strategies such as implementing end-to-end encryption and access controls to secure IoT data and devices, adopting interoperability standards (e.g., MQTT, CoAP) for seamless communication between heterogeneous IoT devices and platforms, and using device management platforms or IoT device management protocols (e.g., MQTT-SN, LwM2M) for remote device provisioning, monitoring, and firmware updates.

Q4: How do you design for fault tolerance and reliability in IoT platforms?

A4: Designing for fault tolerance and reliability in IoT platforms involves redundancy, data replication, and failover mechanisms. Candidates may discuss techniques such as deploying redundant IoT gateways and edge computing nodes to ensure high availability of data processing and analysis, setting up data replication and synchronization processes to maintain data consistency and durability across distributed nodes or cloud regions, and implementing automated failover and recovery procedures to handle node failures or network disruptions and ensure uninterrupted IoT data collection and processing.

Chapter 50: Building Scalable Content Management Systems

Q1: What are the essential components to consider when building a scalable content management system (CMS)?

A1: Building a scalable content management system involves considering key components such as content repositories, user management systems, access control mechanisms, caching layers, and content delivery networks (CDNs). These components enable efficient content creation, storage, retrieval, and delivery while accommodating increasing user traffic and content volumes.

Q2: How do you ensure scalability in content management system design?

A2: Ensuring scalability in content management system design involves employing distributed architectures, horizontal scaling, and caching strategies. Candidates may discuss techniques such as using distributed databases or storage solutions for storing and retrieving content, implementing load balancers and auto-scaling mechanisms to distribute traffic across multiple server instances, and utilizing caching layers or CDNs to cache frequently accessed content and improve response times for users.

Q3: What challenges might arise when building scalable content management systems, and how can they be addressed?

A3: Challenges associated with building scalable content management systems include content versioning, data consistency, and search indexing. Candidates may discuss strategies such as implementing content version control mechanisms to manage revisions and updates to content, using distributed locking or consensus protocols to ensure data consistency across distributed content repositories, and employing search indexing platforms or search as a service (SaaS) solutions for efficient content indexing and retrieval.

Q4: How do you design for fault tolerance and reliability in content management systems?

A4: Designing for fault tolerance and reliability in content management systems involves redundancy, data replication, and disaster recovery planning. Candidates may discuss techniques such as deploying redundant content servers and storage clusters to ensure high availability of content and services, setting up data replication and backup processes to maintain data durability and recoverability in the event of hardware failures or data corruption, and implementing failover mechanisms and load balancing strategies to handle traffic spikes and ensure continuous content delivery and availability.

Chapter 51: Designing for Cross-Platform Compatibility

Q1: What factors should be considered when designing for cross-platform compatibility?

A1: When designing for cross-platform compatibility, factors such as operating systems, devices, screen sizes, input methods, and user interface guidelines need to be considered. These factors ensure that the application or system functions seamlessly across different platforms, providing a consistent user experience for all users.

Q2: How do you ensure cross-platform compatibility in system design?

A2: Ensuring cross-platform compatibility in system design involves using platform-agnostic technologies, responsive design principles, and compatibility testing. Candidates may discuss approaches such as developing web-based applications using HTML5, CSS3, and JavaScript for broad compatibility across desktop and mobile platforms, employing responsive design techniques to adapt the user interface layout and content based on the device screen size and orientation, and conducting compatibility testing across multiple platforms and devices to identify and address any compatibility issues proactively.

Q3: What challenges might arise when designing for cross-platform compatibility, and how can they be addressed?

A3: Challenges associated with designing for cross-platform compatibility include platform-specific features, performance optimization, and user experience consistency. Candidates may discuss strategies such as implementing feature detection and fallback mechanisms to handle platform-specific features or limitations gracefully, optimizing performance and resource usage for each target platform through code profiling and optimization techniques, and maintaining consistent user interface elements and interaction patterns across different platforms to provide a unified user experience.

Q4: How do you prioritize platform support when designing for cross-platform compatibility?

A4: Prioritizing platform support when designing for cross-platform compatibility involves considering factors such as target audience demographics, market share, and business requirements. Candidates may discuss techniques such as conducting market research to identify the most prevalent platforms among the target audience, analyzing user feedback and usage metrics to prioritize platform support based on user preferences and behavior, and aligning platform support decisions with the organization's strategic goals and product roadmap to maximize impact and return on investment.

Chapter 52: System Design for Financial Trading Systems

Q1: What are the critical components to consider when designing a financial trading system?

A1: Designing a financial trading system involves considering critical components such as order management, trade execution, risk management, market data feeds, compliance, and reporting. These components facilitate the efficient execution of trades, real-time monitoring of market conditions, risk mitigation, and regulatory compliance in the financial markets.

Q2: How do you ensure low-latency and high-throughput performance in financial trading system design?

A2: Ensuring low-latency and high-throughput performance in financial trading system design involves leveraging high-performance computing, optimized network protocols, and proximity hosting. Candidates may discuss techniques such as using low-latency messaging protocols (e.g., FIX, FAST) for real-time data transmission, deploying colocation services to reduce network latency between trading systems and exchanges, and optimizing algorithms and data processing pipelines for minimal processing latency and maximum throughput.

Q3: What challenges might arise when designing financial trading systems, and how can they be addressed?

A3: Challenges associated with designing financial trading systems include market volatility, regulatory compliance, and cybersecurity risks. Candidates may discuss strategies such as implementing circuit breakers and risk controls to mitigate the impact of sudden market fluctuations and prevent excessive trading risks, adhering to regulatory requirements (e.g., SEC, MiFID II) for trade reporting, transaction monitoring, and client data protection, and implementing robust cybersecurity measures (e.g., encryption, multi-factor authentication) to safeguard sensitive financial data and prevent unauthorized access or data breaches.

Q4: How do you design for fault tolerance and reliability in financial trading systems?

A4: Designing for fault tolerance and reliability in financial trading systems involves redundancy, failover mechanisms, and disaster recovery planning. Candidates may discuss techniques such as deploying redundant trading servers and data centers to ensure high availability and fault tolerance, setting up automated failover and recovery processes to handle server failures or network disruptions, and implementing backup and data replication strategies for disaster recovery and business continuity in the event of system failures or catastrophic events.

Chapter 53: Building Scalable Recommendation Systems

Q1: What are the essential components to consider when building a scalable recommendation system?

A1: Building a scalable recommendation system involves considering key components such as data ingestion pipelines, recommendation algorithms, user modeling, recommendation storage, and real-time serving layers. These components work together to collect user interactions, analyze preferences, generate personalized recommendations, and serve them to users in real-time.

Q2: How do you ensure scalability in recommendation system design?

A2: Ensuring scalability in recommendation system design involves employing distributed architectures, parallel processing, and caching mechanisms. Candidates may discuss approaches such as using distributed databases or storage solutions for storing and accessing user and item data, implementing distributed recommendation algorithms that can operate in parallel across multiple nodes, and leveraging caching layers or in-memory databases to cache precomputed recommendations and improve response times for users.

Q3: What challenges might arise when building scalable recommendation systems, and how can they be addressed?

A3: Challenges associated with building scalable recommendation systems include cold-start problems, data sparsity, and model training complexity. Candidates may discuss strategies such as using hybrid recommendation approaches that combine collaborative filtering and content-based methods to mitigate cold-start problems and improve recommendation accuracy, employing data preprocessing and feature engineering techniques to handle sparse data and extract meaningful user and item features, and using distributed computing frameworks and model parallelization techniques to train complex recommendation models efficiently on large-scale datasets.

Q4: How do you design for fault tolerance and reliability in recommendation systems?

A4: Designing for fault tolerance and reliability in recommendation systems involves redundancy, data replication, and error recovery mechanisms. Candidates may discuss techniques such as deploying redundant recommendation servers and storage clusters to ensure high availability of recommendation services, setting up data replication and synchronization processes to maintain data consistency and durability across distributed nodes or cloud regions, and implementing fault detection and recovery mechanisms (e.g., circuit breakers, retry strategies) to handle service failures or network disruptions and ensure continuous recommendation serving and user engagement.

Chapter 54: Designing for Regulatory Compliance

Q1: What considerations are important when designing for regulatory compliance in a system?

A1: Designing for regulatory compliance requires careful consideration of relevant laws, regulations, and industry standards pertaining to data privacy, security, financial transactions, and consumer protection. It involves implementing appropriate controls, audit trails, encryption mechanisms, and access restrictions to ensure compliance with legal requirements and regulatory frameworks.

Q2: How do you ensure data privacy and security in system design to meet regulatory standards?

A2: Ensuring data privacy and security in system design to meet regulatory standards involves implementing encryption techniques, access controls, data masking, and anonymization mechanisms. Candidates may discuss strategies such as encrypting sensitive data at rest and in transit, enforcing role-based access controls to restrict data access based on user roles and permissions, and anonymizing or pseudonymizing personally identifiable information (PII) to protect user privacy and comply with data protection regulations like GDPR or CCPA.

Q3: What challenges might arise when designing for regulatory compliance, and how can they be addressed?

A3: Challenges associated with designing for regulatory compliance include interpreting complex legal requirements, ensuring ongoing compliance, and managing regulatory changes. Candidates may discuss strategies such as engaging legal experts or compliance officers to interpret and translate regulatory requirements into technical specifications, implementing robust compliance monitoring and auditing processes to track adherence to regulatory standards and detect any deviations or violations, and establishing procedures for timely updates and revisions to system designs and controls in response to changes in regulations or compliance obligations.

Q4: How do you design for auditability and accountability in systems to meet regulatory requirements?

A4: Designing for auditability and accountability in systems to meet regulatory requirements involves maintaining detailed audit trails, logs, and documentation, as well as implementing transparency and traceability mechanisms. Candidates may discuss techniques such as logging all user interactions, system activities, and data access events to create an audit trail for compliance auditing and forensic analysis, providing mechanisms for administrators or auditors to review and analyze system logs and audit trails to verify compliance with regulatory standards, and documenting system architecture, design decisions, and control mechanisms to demonstrate accountability and compliance with regulatory requirements during audits or inspections.

Chapter 55: System Design for Digital Asset Management

Q1: What are the essential components to consider when designing a digital asset management system?

A1: Designing a digital asset management system involves considering key components such as asset ingestion pipelines, metadata management, storage infrastructure, access controls, search capabilities, and asset delivery mechanisms. These components enable the efficient storage, organization, retrieval, and distribution of digital assets such as images, videos, documents, and multimedia content.

Q2: How do you ensure scalability and performance in digital asset management system design?

A2: Ensuring scalability and performance in digital asset management system design involves leveraging distributed architectures, caching strategies, and content delivery networks (CDNs). Candidates may discuss approaches such as using distributed storage solutions or object storage platforms for storing and accessing digital assets at scale, implementing caching layers or in-memory databases to cache frequently accessed assets and metadata for improved performance, and utilizing CDNs for efficient content delivery and distribution to users globally.

Q3: What challenges might arise when designing digital asset management systems, and how can they be addressed?

A3: Challenges associated with designing digital asset management systems include metadata management, asset versioning, and asset lifecycle management. Candidates may discuss strategies such as implementing robust metadata schemas and indexing mechanisms to categorize and organize assets effectively, using version control systems or asset versioning techniques to manage revisions and updates to digital assets over time, and establishing workflows and policies for asset lifecycle management, including creation, approval, archiving, and deletion, to ensure compliance with regulatory requirements and business rules.

Q4: How do you design for data security and access control in digital asset management systems?

A4: Designing for data security and access control in digital asset management systems involves implementing encryption, access controls, and user authentication mechanisms. Candidates may discuss techniques such as encrypting sensitive assets at rest and in transit to protect against unauthorized access or data breaches, enforcing role-based access controls to restrict access to assets based on user roles and permissions, and implementing single sign-on (SSO) or multi-factor authentication (MFA) for secure user authentication and identity verification.

Chapter 56: Building Scalable Online Learning Platforms

Q1: What are the fundamental components to consider when building a scalable online learning platform?

A1: Building a scalable online learning platform involves considering key components such as user management, content management, course delivery, assessment tools, and performance tracking. These components facilitate the creation, delivery, and management of educational content, interactions with learners, and tracking of learner progress and achievements.

Q2: How do you ensure scalability and performance in online learning platform design?

A2: Ensuring scalability and performance in online learning platform design involves leveraging cloud infrastructure, content delivery networks (CDNs), and asynchronous processing. Candidates may discuss approaches such as using scalable cloud computing services for dynamic resource allocation and auto-scaling based on user demand, leveraging CDNs to distribute content and reduce latency for users worldwide, and implementing asynchronous processing for tasks such as content rendering, user authentication, and data processing to improve platform responsiveness and scalability.

Q3: What challenges might arise when building scalable online learning platforms, and how can they be addressed?

A3: Challenges associated with building scalable online learning platforms include content personalization, learner engagement, and data privacy. Candidates may discuss strategies such as implementing recommendation algorithms and adaptive learning techniques to personalize content and tailor learning experiences to individual learner preferences and proficiency levels, designing interactive and gamified learning activities to enhance learner engagement and motivation, and ensuring compliance with data privacy regulations (e.g., GDPR, COPPA) by implementing robust data protection measures, obtaining user consent for data processing, and providing transparency about data collection and usage practices.

Q4: How do you design for interactivity and collaboration in online learning platforms?

A4: Designing for interactivity and collaboration in online learning platforms involves integrating communication tools, discussion forums, and collaborative features. Candidates may discuss techniques such as incorporating real-time chat, video conferencing, and messaging functionalities to enable synchronous communication and collaboration among learners and instructors, implementing discussion forums, wikis, and peer review mechanisms to facilitate asynchronous collaboration and knowledge sharing, and integrating interactive multimedia elements, simulations, and virtual labs to create engaging and interactive learning experiences for learners.

Chapter 57: Designing for Privacy and Data Protection

Q1: What factors should be considered when designing for privacy and data protection in a system?

A1: Designing for privacy and data protection involves considering factors such as data encryption, access controls, data anonymization, regulatory compliance, and user consent. These factors ensure that sensitive user information is adequately protected against unauthorized access, misuse, and data breaches, while also complying with relevant data protection laws and regulations.

Q2: How do you ensure data privacy and protection in system design?

A2: Ensuring data privacy and protection in system design involves implementing encryption techniques, access controls, and data minimization practices. Candidates may discuss approaches such as encrypting sensitive data at rest and in transit to prevent unauthorized access, enforcing role-based access controls and least privilege principles to restrict data access based on user roles and permissions, and minimizing the collection and storage of personally identifiable information (PII) to reduce the risk of data exposure and misuse.

Q3: What challenges might arise when designing for privacy and data protection, and how can they be addressed?

A3: Challenges associated with designing for privacy and data protection include regulatory compliance, data governance, and data lifecycle management. Candidates may discuss strategies such as conducting privacy impact assessments (PIAs) to identify and mitigate privacy risks associated with system design and implementation, implementing data classification and retention policies to govern the collection, storage, and disposal of sensitive data in accordance with legal requirements, and establishing data breach response plans and incident response procedures to detect, investigate, and respond to security incidents and data breaches promptly.

Q4: How do you design for transparency and user control over their data in systems?

A4: Designing for transparency and user control over their data in systems involves providing clear information about data collection and usage practices, as well as giving users options to manage their privacy preferences and consent settings. Candidates may discuss techniques such as providing privacy notices and consent forms that explain how user data will be collected, processed, and shared, offering granular privacy settings and preferences that allow users to control the types of data collected and the purposes for which it is used, and implementing user-friendly interfaces and tools for accessing, reviewing, and deleting personal data stored in the system.

Chapter 58: System Design for Fleet Management Systems

Q1: What are the essential components to consider when designing a fleet management system?

A1: Designing a fleet management system involves considering key components such as vehicle tracking, route optimization, driver management, maintenance scheduling, and reporting and analytics. These components enable efficient monitoring, operation, and maintenance of a fleet of vehicles, ensuring optimal performance and productivity.

Q2: How do you ensure real-time tracking and monitoring in fleet management system design?

A2: Ensuring real-time tracking and monitoring in fleet management system design involves leveraging GPS technology, telemetry sensors, and wireless communication networks. Candidates may discuss approaches such as equipping vehicles with GPS trackers or telematics devices to collect location and sensor data in real-time, using cellular or satellite networks for data transmission and communication between vehicles and central servers, and implementing event-driven architectures or message queuing systems for processing and analyzing streaming telemetry data for real-time monitoring and decision-making.

Q3: What challenges might arise when designing fleet management systems, and how can they be addressed?

A3: Challenges associated with designing fleet management systems include data integration, interoperability, and scalability. Candidates may discuss strategies such as integrating data from disparate sources such as vehicle sensors, GPS devices, and backend systems for centralized monitoring and analysis, adopting standardized communication protocols (e.g., CAN bus, OBD-II) for interoperability between different vehicle makes and models, and designing scalable architectures with distributed processing and storage capabilities to handle large volumes of telemetry data and accommodate fleet expansion and growth.

Q4: How do you design for driver safety and compliance in fleet management systems?

A4: Designing for driver safety and compliance in fleet management systems involves implementing driver behavior monitoring, compliance tracking, and safety alerts. Candidates may discuss techniques such as installing driver-facing cameras or telematics devices to monitor driver behavior and identify unsafe practices such as speeding, harsh braking, or distracted driving, integrating compliance management features to track driver hours-of-service (HOS) compliance, vehicle inspections, and regulatory requirements (e.g., FMCSA regulations for commercial fleets), and configuring real-time alerts and notifications to alert drivers and fleet managers of safety violations or compliance issues for timely intervention and corrective action.

Chapter 59: Building Scalable Customer Relationship Management (CRM) Systems

Q1: What are the critical components to consider when building a scalable customer relationship management (CRM) system?

A1: Building a scalable CRM system involves considering key components such as customer data management, sales automation, marketing automation, customer service, and analytics. These components facilitate the efficient management of customer interactions, leads, opportunities, and campaigns across various touchpoints, enabling businesses to nurture relationships and drive sales growth.

Q2: How do you ensure scalability and performance in CRM system design?

A2: Ensuring scalability and performance in CRM system design involves leveraging distributed architectures, data partitioning, and caching mechanisms. Candidates may discuss approaches such as using distributed databases or cloud-based solutions for storing and accessing customer data at scale, implementing data partitioning strategies (e.g., sharding) to distribute data across multiple database instances and improve query performance, and deploying caching layers or in-memory databases to cache frequently accessed data and improve response times for users.

Q3: What challenges might arise when building scalable CRM systems, and how can they be addressed?

A3: Challenges associated with building scalable CRM systems include data integration, user concurrency, and data consistency. Candidates may discuss strategies such as implementing data integration and synchronization mechanisms to aggregate and reconcile customer data from disparate sources (e.g., CRM applications, marketing automation platforms, ERP systems), using database replication and distributed transaction processing techniques to ensure data consistency and integrity across distributed databases, and optimizing database indexing and query performance to handle concurrent user access and data processing loads efficiently.

Q4: How do you design for personalized customer experiences in CRM systems?

A4: Designing for personalized customer experiences in CRM systems involves leveraging customer segmentation, predictive analytics, and marketing automation capabilities. Candidates may discuss techniques such as creating customer segments based on demographics, behavior, or preferences to target personalized marketing campaigns and offers, using predictive analytics models to anticipate customer needs and recommend relevant products or services, and integrating marketing automation workflows to deliver personalized content and messages across multiple channels (e.g., email, social media, mobile) based on customer interactions and engagement history.

Chapter 60: Designing for Adaptive Streaming Technologies

Q1: What are the essential components to consider when designing for adaptive streaming technologies?

A1: Designing for adaptive streaming technologies involves considering key components such as video encoding, content delivery networks (CDNs), client-side players, and adaptive bitrate (ABR) algorithms. These components enable the efficient delivery of multimedia content over the internet, adjusting video quality and bitrate dynamically based on network conditions and device capabilities to provide a seamless viewing experience for users.

Q2: How do you ensure scalability and performance in adaptive streaming system design?

A2: Ensuring scalability and performance in adaptive streaming system design involves leveraging scalable encoding solutions, CDN caching, and dynamic bitrate adaptation. Candidates may discuss approaches such as using cloud-based encoding services or distributed encoding farms for parallel processing of video content to accommodate increasing demand, deploying CDN caching servers at strategic locations to cache video segments and reduce latency for users, and implementing adaptive bitrate algorithms that monitor network conditions and device capabilities to adjust video quality and bitrate dynamically for optimal playback performance.

Q3: What challenges might arise when designing for adaptive streaming technologies, and how can they be addressed?

A3: Challenges associated with designing for adaptive streaming technologies include latency, video quality, and device compatibility. Candidates may discuss strategies such as implementing low-latency streaming protocols (e.g., HLS Low-Latency, CMAF) and chunked transfer encoding to reduce latency and improve real-time streaming performance, optimizing video encoding parameters and transcoding presets to balance video quality and file size for different bitrate renditions, and testing and validating adaptive streaming solutions across various devices, browsers, and network conditions to ensure compatibility and consistent playback experiences for users.

Q4: How do you design for content protection and digital rights management (DRM) in adaptive streaming systems?

A4: Designing for content protection and DRM in adaptive streaming systems involves implementing encryption, tokenization, and license management mechanisms. Candidates may discuss techniques such as encrypting video content using industry-standard encryption algorithms (e.g., AES) to protect against unauthorized access or piracy, tokenizing playback requests and generating short-lived access tokens to control access to encrypted content and prevent replay attacks, and integrating DRM solutions or third-party DRM providers to manage content licenses, enforce access controls, and enable secure playback of protected content on authorized devices and players.

Chapter 61: System Design for Supply Chain Management

Q1: What are the critical components to consider when designing a supply chain management system?

A1: Designing a supply chain management system involves considering key components such as inventory management, order fulfillment, logistics, demand forecasting, and supplier relationship management. These components enable businesses to optimize the flow of goods, materials, and information across the supply chain, from sourcing raw materials to delivering finished products to customers.

Q2: How do you ensure scalability and efficiency in supply chain management system design?

A2: Ensuring scalability and efficiency in supply chain management system design involves leveraging automation, real-time visibility, and data analytics. Candidates may discuss approaches such as using automated inventory management systems and robotic process automation (RPA) for streamlining order processing and fulfillment tasks, implementing supply chain visibility solutions that provide real-time tracking and monitoring of inventory levels, shipments, and delivery status, and employing data analytics and machine learning algorithms to analyze historical data, predict demand patterns, and optimize inventory levels and logistics operations for cost savings and improved efficiency.

Q3: What challenges might arise when designing supply chain management systems, and how can they be addressed?

A3: Challenges associated with designing supply chain management systems include supply chain complexity, data integration, and global logistics coordination. Candidates may discuss strategies such as modeling supply chain networks using graph theory and network optimization techniques to identify bottlenecks, optimize routing, and improve supply chain resilience, implementing data integration platforms and APIs for connecting disparate systems and data sources across the supply chain ecosystem, and collaborating with logistics partners and leveraging advanced tracking technologies (e.g., IoT sensors, RFID tags) to enhance visibility and coordination in global supply chain operations.

Q4: How do you design for supply chain resilience and risk management in supply chain management systems?

A4: Designing for supply chain resilience and risk management in supply chain management systems involves implementing contingency planning, supplier diversification, and supply chain analytics. Candidates may discuss techniques such as conducting risk assessments and scenario planning to identify potential supply chain disruptions and develop mitigation strategies and alternative sourcing options, establishing supplier risk management programs and supplier scorecards to evaluate supplier performance, reliability, and resilience, and using supply chain analytics and simulation models to simulate and analyze different risk scenarios, assess their potential impact on supply chain operations, and optimize risk mitigation strategies and inventory levels accordingly.

Chapter 62: Building Scalable Geographic Information Systems (GIS)

Q1: What are the essential components to consider when building a scalable Geographic Information System (GIS)?

A1: Building a scalable GIS involves considering key components such as spatial data storage, data visualization tools, geoprocessing capabilities, and spatial analysis algorithms. These components enable the collection, storage, analysis, and visualization of geographic data, including maps, satellite imagery, and spatial datasets, to support various applications such as urban planning, environmental monitoring, and location-based services.

Q2: How do you ensure scalability and performance in GIS system design?

A2: Ensuring scalability and performance in GIS system design involves leveraging distributed architectures, spatial indexing techniques, and caching mechanisms. Candidates may discuss approaches such as using distributed databases or cloud-based storage solutions for storing and accessing spatial data at scale, implementing spatial indexing structures (e.g., R-tree, quadtree) to optimize spatial queries and data retrieval, and deploying caching layers or in-memory databases to cache frequently accessed spatial data and improve response times for users.

Q3: What challenges might arise when building scalable GIS systems, and how can they be addressed?

A3: Challenges associated with building scalable GIS systems include data interoperability, computational complexity, and data visualization. Candidates may discuss strategies such as implementing data interoperability standards (e.g., OGC standards) and data exchange formats (e.g., GeoJSON, Shapefile) to facilitate data sharing and integration across different GIS platforms and systems, optimizing spatial algorithms and geoprocessing workflows for parallel execution and distributed computing environments to handle large-scale spatial analysis tasks efficiently, and using scalable visualization techniques (e.g., vector tiles, raster tiling) and client-side rendering libraries (e.g., Mapbox, Leaflet) to render and display complex geographic datasets and maps seamlessly in web and mobile applications.

Q4: How do you design for spatial data integrity and consistency in GIS systems?

A4: Designing for spatial data integrity and consistency in GIS systems involves implementing data validation, quality control, and versioning mechanisms. Candidates may discuss techniques such as enforcing data validation rules and constraints to ensure the accuracy and completeness of spatial data during data entry and updates, conducting data quality checks and audits to identify and correct errors or anomalies in spatial datasets, and implementing version control and revision history tracking features to manage changes to spatial data and maintain data lineage, audit trails, and historical snapshots for traceability and accountability purposes.

Chapter 63: Designing for Cloud-Native Applications

Q1: What are the key principles to consider when designing cloud-native applications?

A1: Designing cloud-native applications involves adhering to key principles such as microservices architecture, containerization, infrastructure as code (IaC), and continuous integration/continuous deployment (CI/CD). These principles enable applications to be developed, deployed, and scaled more efficiently in cloud environments, promoting agility, scalability, and resilience.

Q2: How do you ensure scalability and resilience in cloud-native application design?

A2: Ensuring scalability and resilience in cloud-native application design involves leveraging container orchestration platforms (e.g., Kubernetes), autoscaling mechanisms, and distributed architectures. Candidates may discuss approaches such as deploying microservices-based architectures that allow individual components to scale independently, using containerization technologies (e.g., Docker) for packaging and deploying application components consistently across different environments, and implementing fault-tolerant and self-healing patterns (e.g., circuit breakers, retries) to handle failures and ensure high availability of cloud-native applications.

Q3: What challenges might arise when designing cloud-native applications, and how can they be addressed?

A3: Challenges associated with designing cloud-native applications include complexity, service dependencies, and security concerns. Candidates may discuss strategies such as breaking down monolithic applications into smaller, more manageable microservices to reduce complexity and improve modularity, implementing service meshes or API gateways to manage communication and interactions between microservices and external services, and adopting security best practices such as encryption, identity and access management (IAM), and network segmentation to protect cloud-native applications and data from security threats and breaches.

Q4: How do you design for observability and monitoring in cloud-native applications?

A4: Designing for observability and monitoring in cloud-native applications involves instrumenting applications, logging, and tracing, and using monitoring tools and platforms. Candidates may discuss techniques such as adding telemetry instrumentation to application code to capture metrics, logs, and traces for monitoring and troubleshooting purposes, integrating logging frameworks and log aggregation services (e.g., Elasticsearch, Splunk) to collect and analyze application logs and events, and using distributed tracing systems (e.g., Jaeger, Zipkin) to trace requests and identify performance bottlenecks and latency issues across microservices in cloud-native architectures.

Chapter 64: System Design for Remote Collaboration Tools

Q1: What are the essential components to consider when designing remote collaboration tools?

A1: Designing remote collaboration tools involves considering key components such as real-time communication, document sharing, screen sharing, and collaborative editing features. These components enable users to collaborate effectively with remote colleagues, partners, or clients, facilitating seamless communication, information sharing, and teamwork regardless of geographical locations.

Q2: How do you ensure scalability and performance in remote collaboration tool design?

A2: Ensuring scalability and performance in remote collaboration tool design involves leveraging scalable communication protocols, distributed architectures, and caching mechanisms. Candidates may discuss approaches such as using WebRTC (Web Real-Time Communication) for real-time audio and video communication, deploying microservices-based architectures to scale individual features or modules independently, and implementing caching layers or content delivery networks (CDNs) to optimize content delivery and reduce latency for users in different geographical regions.

Q3: What challenges might arise when designing remote collaboration tools, and how can they be addressed?

A3: Challenges associated with designing remote collaboration tools include network latency, bandwidth constraints, and security concerns. Candidates may discuss strategies such as optimizing network protocols and codecs to minimize latency and bandwidth usage for real-time communication and collaboration, implementing adaptive bitrate streaming and content compression techniques to adjust video quality and optimize bandwidth utilization based on network conditions, and adopting encryption and access controls to protect sensitive information and ensure data privacy and security in remote collaboration sessions.

Q4: How do you design for user experience and accessibility in remote collaboration tools?

A4: Designing for user experience and accessibility in remote collaboration tools involves considering user interfaces, usability features, and assistive technologies. Candidates may discuss techniques such as designing intuitive and user-friendly interfaces with clear navigation and visual cues to facilitate ease of use and adoption for users with varying levels of technical expertise, implementing accessibility features such as keyboard shortcuts, screen reader compatibility, and color contrast settings to accommodate users with disabilities or impairments, and providing multi-platform support and responsive design to ensure seamless access and consistent user experiences across different devices and screen sizes.

Chapter 65: Building Scalable Voice Assistant Platforms

Q1: What are the essential components to consider when building scalable voice assistant platforms?

A1: Building scalable voice assistant platforms involves considering key components such as natural language processing (NLP), speech recognition, dialogue management, and integration with third-party services. These components enable voice assistants to understand user queries, generate appropriate responses, and perform tasks or retrieve information from external systems, providing users with personalized and interactive experiences.

Q2: How do you ensure scalability and performance in voice assistant platform design?

A2: Ensuring scalability and performance in voice assistant platform design involves leveraging cloud-based services, distributed architectures, and optimization techniques. Candidates may discuss approaches such as using cloud-based NLP and speech recognition APIs for processing user queries and audio input, deploying microservices-based architectures to scale individual components or functionalities independently, and optimizing algorithms and data structures to improve response times and minimize latency for real-time interactions with voice assistants.

Q3: What challenges might arise when building scalable voice assistant platforms, and how can they be addressed?

A3: Challenges associated with building scalable voice assistant platforms include language understanding, context management, and privacy concerns. Candidates may discuss strategies such as training and fine-tuning NLP models and speech recognition algorithms to improve language understanding and accuracy in interpreting user queries and intents, implementing context-aware dialogue management techniques to maintain conversational context and handle multi-turn interactions seamlessly, and incorporating privacy-by-design principles and user consent mechanisms to protect user data and ensure compliance with data privacy regulations (e.g., GDPR, CCPA).

Q4: How do you design for personalized user experiences in voice assistant platforms?

A4: Designing for personalized user experiences in voice assistant platforms involves user profiling, personalization algorithms, and integration with user preferences and history. Candidates may discuss techniques such as collecting and analyzing user interactions and feedback to create user profiles and preferences, using machine learning algorithms to personalize responses and recommendations based on user preferences, behavior, and context, and integrating with user accounts and historical data from other applications or services (e.g., calendar, music preferences) to provide tailored and contextually relevant experiences for individual users.

Chapter 66: Designing for Edge Computing Architectures

Q1: What are the essential components to consider when designing edge computing architectures?

A1: Designing edge computing architectures involves considering key components such as edge nodes, edge gateways, edge servers, and edge applications. These components enable the processing, storage, and analysis of data closer to the source or end-users, reducing latency, bandwidth usage, and dependence on centralized cloud infrastructure.

Q2: How do you ensure scalability and performance in edge computing architecture design?

A2: Ensuring scalability and performance in edge computing architecture design involves optimizing resource allocation, workload distribution, and data processing at the edge. Candidates may discuss approaches such as deploying containerized or lightweight virtualization technologies for efficient resource utilization and isolation, implementing edge caching and content delivery mechanisms to reduce latency and improve data access times, and leveraging distributed computing paradigms (e.g., edge-to-edge communication, federated learning) to distribute computation and data processing tasks across edge nodes and devices for parallel execution and scalability.

Q3: What challenges might arise when designing edge computing architectures, and how can they be addressed?

A3: Challenges associated with designing edge computing architectures include network connectivity, device heterogeneity, and data security. Candidates may discuss strategies such as optimizing network protocols and bandwidth management techniques to accommodate intermittent or low-bandwidth network connections in edge environments, implementing device management and orchestration frameworks to manage and coordinate heterogeneous edge devices and platforms effectively, and adopting security-by-design principles and encryption techniques to protect sensitive data and ensure secure communication and data exchange between edge nodes and central systems.

Q4: How do you design for resilience and fault tolerance in edge computing architectures?

A4: Designing for resilience and fault tolerance in edge computing architectures involves implementing redundancy, failover mechanisms, and decentralized processing. Candidates may discuss techniques such as deploying redundant edge nodes and gateway clusters to provide high availability and fault tolerance in edge deployments, using distributed consensus protocols (e.g., Raft, Paxos) or blockchain-based approaches for consensus and data replication across edge nodes to ensure data consistency and fault tolerance, and designing decentralized edge applications with local decision-making capabilities and offline operation modes to mitigate single points of failure and dependency on centralized infrastructure or cloud services.

Chapter 67: System Design for Content Recommendation Engines

Q1: What are the key components to consider when designing content recommendation engines?

A1: Designing content recommendation engines involves considering key components such as data collection, user profiling, recommendation algorithms, and content delivery. These components enable the analysis of user preferences, behavior, and interactions to generate personalized recommendations and deliver relevant content to users based on their interests and preferences.

Q2: How do you ensure scalability and performance in content recommendation engine design?

A2: Ensuring scalability and performance in content recommendation engine design involves leveraging scalable data processing and machine learning technologies. Candidates may discuss approaches such as using distributed data storage and processing frameworks (e.g., Apache Hadoop, Apache Spark) for analyzing large volumes of user data and generating recommendations at scale, deploying machine learning models and algorithms in parallel across distributed computing environments for efficient training and inference, and implementing caching and content delivery networks (CDNs) to optimize recommendation delivery and reduce latency for users.

Q3: What challenges might arise when designing content recommendation engines, and how can they be addressed?

A3: Challenges associated with designing content recommendation engines include data sparsity, cold start problems, and algorithmic biases. Candidates may discuss strategies such as leveraging collaborative filtering techniques and matrix factorization methods to address data sparsity and generate accurate recommendations based on user-item interactions and similarities, implementing hybrid recommendation approaches that combine content-based and collaborative filtering methods to handle cold start scenarios and recommend items to new or inactive users, and using fairness-aware algorithms and bias mitigation techniques to reduce algorithmic biases and ensure diverse and inclusive recommendations for all users.

Q4: How do you design for user engagement and personalization in content recommendation engines?

A4: Designing for user engagement and personalization in content recommendation engines involves tailoring recommendations to individual user preferences and optimizing recommendation delivery channels. Candidates may discuss techniques such as analyzing user feedback and engagement metrics to iteratively refine recommendation models and algorithms and improve recommendation accuracy and relevance over time, implementing context-aware recommendation strategies that consider user context (e.g., location, time, device) and content context (e.g., genre, popularity) to deliver timely and relevant recommendations, and integrating with multi-channel delivery platforms (e.g., websites, mobile apps, smart devices) to provide personalized recommendations across different touchpoints and devices based on user interactions and preferences.

Chapter 68: Building Scalable Data Analytics Platforms

Q1: What are the essential components to consider when building scalable data analytics platforms?

A1: Building scalable data analytics platforms involves considering key components such as data ingestion, storage, processing, and visualization. These components enable organizations to collect, store, analyze, and visualize large volumes of data efficiently, enabling data-driven decision-making and insights generation.

Q2: How do you ensure scalability and performance in data analytics platform design?

A2: Ensuring scalability and performance in data analytics platform design involves leveraging distributed computing frameworks, parallel processing, and optimization techniques. Candidates may discuss approaches such as using distributed storage systems (e.g., Hadoop Distributed File System, Amazon S3) for storing and accessing large datasets, deploying distributed processing frameworks (e.g., Apache Spark, Apache Flink) for parallel data processing and computation, and optimizing data pipelines and workflows for efficient data transformation and analysis.

Q3: What challenges might arise when building scalable data analytics platforms, and how can they be addressed?

A3: Challenges associated with building scalable data analytics platforms include data integration, data quality, and resource contention. Candidates may discuss strategies such as implementing data integration and ETL (Extract, Transform, Load) processes to aggregate and cleanse data from disparate sources, establishing data governance policies and data quality checks to ensure data accuracy and consistency, and optimizing resource utilization and workload scheduling to mitigate resource contention and bottlenecks in distributed computing environments.

Q4: How do you design for real-time analytics and streaming data processing in data analytics platforms?

A4: Designing for real-time analytics and streaming data processing in data analytics platforms involves implementing stream processing frameworks, event-driven architectures, and real-time visualization tools. Candidates may discuss techniques such as using stream processing engines (e.g., Apache Kafka Streams, Apache Flink) for processing and analyzing data streams in real-time, designing event-driven architectures with message queues and event brokers to handle asynchronous data processing and event-driven workflows, and integrating with real-time visualization and dashboarding tools (e.g., Kibana, Grafana) to monitor and visualize streaming data and analytics results in real-time for actionable insights and decision-making.

Chapter 69: Designing for Multi-Tenancy and Isolation

Q1: What are the key considerations when designing for multi-tenancy and isolation in a system?

A1: Designing for multi-tenancy and isolation involves considering factors such as data segregation, resource sharing, access control, and performance isolation. These considerations ensure that multiple tenants (users or organizations) can securely share the same system while maintaining data privacy, security, and performance requirements.

Q2: How do you ensure data isolation and privacy between tenants in a multi-tenant system?

A2: Ensuring data isolation and privacy between tenants in a multi-tenant system involves implementing robust data segmentation, access controls, and encryption mechanisms. Candidates may discuss approaches such as using database schema per tenant or row-level access controls to enforce data segregation, implementing role-based access control (RBAC) and attribute-based access control (ABAC) to restrict access to tenant-specific data, and encrypting sensitive data at rest and in transit to protect against unauthorized access and data breaches.

Q3: What strategies can be employed to achieve resource sharing and optimization in a multi-tenant environment?

A3: Strategies to achieve resource sharing and optimization in a multi-tenant environment include resource pooling, resource quotas, and resource prioritization. Candidates may discuss techniques such as pooling computational resources (e.g., CPU, memory, storage) across multiple tenants to maximize resource utilization, setting resource quotas or limits for each tenant to prevent resource contention and ensure fair resource allocation, and implementing workload prioritization policies to allocate resources based on tenant priorities, service level agreements (SLAs), or usage patterns.

Q4: How do you address performance isolation and scalability challenges in a multi-tenant system?

A4: Addressing performance isolation and scalability challenges in a multi-tenant system involves implementing resource throttling, workload isolation, and performance monitoring. Candidates may discuss methods such as rate limiting or throttling requests from individual tenants to prevent resource exhaustion and ensure equitable resource sharing, isolating tenant workloads or containers to minimize interference and noisy neighbor effects, and monitoring resource usage and performance metrics (e.g., response times, throughput) to identify performance bottlenecks and optimize resource allocation and scaling strategies for improved scalability and performance.

Chapter 70: System Design for Online Travel Booking Systems

Q1: What are the critical components to consider when designing an online travel booking system?

A1: Designing an online travel booking system involves considering key components such as search and booking functionality, inventory management, payment processing, and integration with third-party travel suppliers (e.g., airlines, hotels, car rental agencies). These components enable users to search for travel options, compare prices, make reservations, and complete bookings seamlessly within a single platform.

Q2: How do you ensure scalability and performance in an online travel booking system design?

A2: Ensuring scalability and performance in an online travel booking system design involves optimizing database queries, caching frequently accessed data, and leveraging distributed architectures. Candidates may discuss approaches such as using horizontal scaling and load balancing techniques to distribute traffic across multiple servers or microservices, implementing caching layers or content delivery networks (CDNs) to improve response times and reduce latency for users, and optimizing database schemas and indexing strategies to optimize query performance and handle large volumes of concurrent user requests.

Q3: What challenges might arise when designing online travel booking systems, and how can they be addressed?

A3: Challenges associated with designing online travel booking systems include data consistency, inventory synchronization, and transaction processing. Candidates may discuss strategies such as implementing distributed transaction management protocols (e.g., two-phase commit) or eventual consistency patterns to maintain data integrity and consistency across distributed systems and services, using message queues or event-driven architectures to synchronize inventory updates and availability status in real-time across different travel suppliers and booking channels, and implementing fault-tolerant and idempotent transaction processing mechanisms to handle transaction failures and ensure data consistency and reliability.

Q4: How do you design for user experience and personalization in online travel booking systems?

A4: Designing for user experience and personalization in online travel booking systems involves designing intuitive user interfaces, providing personalized recommendations, and offering targeted promotions and incentives. Candidates may discuss techniques such as optimizing search and filtering options to help users find relevant travel options quickly and easily, leveraging user profiling and historical booking data to generate personalized recommendations and tailored travel packages based on user preferences and behavior, and integrating with loyalty programs and customer relationship management (CRM) systems to provide personalized offers, discounts, and rewards to loyal customers.

Chapter 71: Building Scalable DevOps Toolchains

Q1: What are the essential components to consider when building scalable DevOps toolchains?

A1: Building scalable DevOps toolchains involves considering key components such as version control systems, continuous integration/continuous deployment (CI/CD) pipelines, configuration management tools, and monitoring and logging solutions. These components enable automation, collaboration, and visibility across the software development and delivery lifecycle, facilitating faster and more reliable software releases.

Q2: How do you ensure scalability and performance in DevOps toolchain design?

A2: Ensuring scalability and performance in DevOps toolchain design involves optimizing workflows, infrastructure provisioning, and automation scripts. Candidates may discuss approaches such as using cloud-based infrastructure or container orchestration platforms (e.g., Kubernetes) to scale CI/CD pipelines and testing environments dynamically based on workload demands, parallelizing build and deployment processes to reduce cycle times and increase throughput, and leveraging infrastructure as code (IaC) and configuration management tools (e.g., Ansible, Terraform) to automate provisioning and configuration tasks and ensure consistency and repeatability across environments.

Q3: What challenges might arise when building scalable DevOps toolchains, and how can they be addressed?

A3: Challenges associated with building scalable DevOps toolchains include complexity, tool integration, and cultural barriers. Candidates may discuss strategies such as adopting modular and extensible architectures for DevOps toolchains to facilitate tool integration and interoperability, implementing best practices such as code reviews, automated testing, and infrastructure as code to enforce quality and consistency standards across development and operations teams, and fostering a culture of collaboration, knowledge sharing, and continuous improvement to address organizational silos and resistance to change.

Q4: How do you design for traceability and auditability in DevOps toolchains?

A4: Designing for traceability and auditability in DevOps toolchains involves logging, monitoring, and version control practices. Candidates may discuss techniques such as instrumenting CI/CD pipelines and deployment workflows to capture detailed logs and metrics at each stage of the software delivery process, integrating with centralized logging and monitoring platforms (e.g., ELK stack, Prometheus) to aggregate and analyze logs and metrics for troubleshooting and performance monitoring purposes, and using version control systems (e.g., Git) and release management tools to track changes, revisions, and deployments across infrastructure and application codebases for traceability and audit trail purposes.

Chapter 72: Designing for Cognitive Computing Systems

Q1: What are the key considerations when designing cognitive computing systems?

A1: Designing cognitive computing systems involves considering factors such as data ingestion, natural language processing (NLP), machine learning (ML), and human-computer interaction. These systems aim to mimic human-like intelligence and decision-making processes, requiring robust algorithms, rich data sources, and seamless user experiences.

Q2: How do you ensure scalability and performance in cognitive computing system design?

A2: Ensuring scalability and performance in cognitive computing system design involves leveraging distributed computing architectures, parallel processing, and optimization techniques. Candidates may discuss approaches such as using distributed data storage and processing frameworks (e.g., Hadoop, Spark) to handle large volumes of data and complex computations, deploying machine learning models and algorithms in parallel across distributed computing environments for efficient training and inference, and optimizing algorithms and data structures for faster processing and lower latency.

Q3: What challenges might arise when designing cognitive computing systems, and how can they be addressed?

A3: Challenges associated with designing cognitive computing systems include data quality, interpretability, and ethical considerations. Candidates may discuss strategies such as implementing data quality checks and preprocessing pipelines to clean and enrich data before feeding it into cognitive systems, designing explainable AI models and decision-making processes to enhance interpretability and trust in cognitive system outputs, and incorporating ethical guidelines and bias mitigation techniques to ensure fairness, transparency, and accountability in cognitive system design and operation.

Q4: How do you design for user interaction and feedback in cognitive computing systems?

A4: Designing for user interaction and feedback in cognitive computing systems involves designing intuitive user interfaces, providing contextual recommendations, and soliciting user feedback loops. Candidates may discuss techniques such as developing conversational interfaces or chatbots with natural language understanding (NLU) capabilities to enable human-like interactions and dialogue with cognitive systems, incorporating personalized recommendations and adaptive learning algorithms to tailor system responses and recommendations based on user preferences and behavior, and integrating feedback mechanisms (e.g., sentiment analysis, user ratings) to collect user input and iteratively improve cognitive system performance and user satisfaction.

Chapter 73: System Design for Autonomous Vehicle Management

Q1: What are the critical components to consider when designing a system for autonomous vehicle management?

A1: Designing a system for autonomous vehicle management involves considering key components such as sensor fusion, decision-making algorithms, communication protocols, and fleet coordination mechanisms. These components enable autonomous vehicles to perceive their surroundings, make real-time decisions, communicate with other vehicles and infrastructure, and operate safely and efficiently in dynamic environments.

Q2: How do you ensure scalability and real-time responsiveness in autonomous vehicle management system design?

A2: Ensuring scalability and real-time responsiveness in autonomous vehicle management system design involves leveraging edge computing, low-latency communication networks, and distributed coordination algorithms. Candidates may discuss approaches such as deploying edge computing nodes or edge AI processing units onboard vehicles to offload computation and reduce latency for real-time perception and decision-making tasks, using low-latency communication protocols (e.g., V2X communication, 5G cellular networks) to enable fast and reliable communication between vehicles and infrastructure, and implementing distributed coordination algorithms (e.g., consensus protocols, multi-agent systems) to coordinate fleet movements and optimize traffic flow in real-time.

Q3: What challenges might arise when designing autonomous vehicle management systems, and how can they be addressed?

A3: Challenges associated with designing autonomous vehicle management systems include safety, cybersecurity, and regulatory compliance. Candidates may discuss strategies such as implementing redundant sensor systems and fail-safe mechanisms to ensure safe operation and mitigate risks of sensor failures or environmental uncertainties, incorporating encryption and authentication protocols to secure vehicle-to-vehicle (V2V) and vehicle-to-infrastructure (V2I) communications and protect against cyber attacks and data breaches, and collaborating with regulatory authorities and industry stakeholders to establish safety standards, certification processes, and legal frameworks for autonomous vehicle deployment and operation.

Q4: How do you design for fleet coordination and optimization in autonomous vehicle management systems?

A4: Designing for fleet coordination and optimization in autonomous vehicle management systems involves developing distributed control algorithms, traffic management strategies, and fleet orchestration platforms. Candidates may discuss techniques such as implementing decentralized decision-making algorithms (e.g., distributed consensus, swarm intelligence) to enable vehicles to coordinate their movements and interactions autonomously without centralized control, designing dynamic routing and traffic management algorithms to optimize fleet operations and minimize congestion, and deploying fleet orchestration platforms or centralized control centers to monitor vehicle status, manage fleet assignments, and dynamically adjust traffic flows and routes based on real-time conditions and objectives.

Chapter 74: Building Scalable Document Management Systems

Q1: What are the essential components to consider when building a scalable document management system?

A1: Building a scalable document management system involves considering key components such as document storage, indexing, retrieval, and access control. These components enable users to store, organize, search, and manage documents efficiently while accommodating growth in data volume and user activity.

Q2: How do you ensure scalability and performance in document management system design?

A2: Ensuring scalability and performance in document management system design involves optimizing data storage, indexing algorithms, and query processing. Candidates may discuss approaches such as using distributed storage systems (e.g., object storage, distributed file systems) to store documents across multiple nodes and scale storage capacity horizontally, implementing indexing and search optimization techniques (e.g., inverted indexes, sharding) to accelerate document retrieval and search queries, and leveraging caching and content delivery networks (CDNs) to reduce latency and improve access times for frequently accessed documents.

Q3: What challenges might arise when building scalable document management systems, and how can they be addressed?

A3: Challenges associated with building scalable document management systems include data consistency, versioning, and access control. Candidates may discuss strategies such as implementing distributed transaction management protocols or eventual consistency patterns to maintain data integrity and consistency across distributed storage systems and replicas, incorporating version control mechanisms and document history tracking to manage document revisions and changes over time, and using role-based access control (RBAC) and fine-grained permissions to enforce access policies and protect sensitive documents from unauthorized access.

Q4: How do you design for document lifecycle management and retention policies in document management systems?

A4: Designing for document lifecycle management and retention policies in document management systems involves defining document workflows, metadata schemas, and retention rules. Candidates may discuss techniques such as modeling document workflows and lifecycle stages (e.g., creation, editing, approval, archiving) to automate document processing and enforce business rules and compliance requirements, defining metadata attributes and tagging conventions to classify and categorize documents based on their content, context, and usage, and implementing retention policies and lifecycle rules to govern document retention periods, archival, and disposal processes in compliance with regulatory and legal requirements.

Chapter 75: Designing for Continuous Integration/Continuous Deployment (CI/CD) Pipelines

Q1: What are the essential components to consider when designing CI/CD pipelines?

A1: Designing CI/CD pipelines involves considering key components such as version control, automated testing, build automation, deployment orchestration, and monitoring. These components enable organizations to automate the software delivery process, from code changes to production deployments, ensuring rapid and reliable delivery of high-quality software.

Q2: How do you ensure scalability and performance in CI/CD pipeline design?

A2: Ensuring scalability and performance in CI/CD pipeline design involves optimizing build processes, parallelizing tasks, and leveraging cloud-based infrastructure. Candidates may discuss approaches such as using distributed build systems or containerized build environments to parallelize build and test execution and reduce build times, optimizing dependency management and artifact caching to minimize network overhead and accelerate build artifact retrieval, and leveraging cloud-based CI/CD services or serverless computing platforms to scale infrastructure resources dynamically based on workload demands and improve overall pipeline performance and reliability.

Q3: What challenges might arise when designing CI/CD pipelines, and how can they be addressed?

A3: Challenges associated with designing CI/CD pipelines include pipeline complexity, environment consistency, and deployment automation. Candidates may discuss strategies such as using pipeline-as-code frameworks (e.g., Jenkins Pipeline, GitLab CI/CD) to define CI/CD workflows and configurations as code and promote versioning, code review, and reuse, implementing infrastructure as code (IaC) and containerization techniques to ensure consistency and repeatability across development, testing, and production environments, and automating deployment orchestration and rollback mechanisms to minimize manual intervention and reduce the risk of deployment failures and downtime.

Q4: How do you design for security and compliance in CI/CD pipelines?

A4: Designing for security and compliance in CI/CD pipelines involves integrating security testing, vulnerability scanning, and compliance checks into the pipeline workflow. Candidates may discuss techniques such as implementing static code analysis and automated security testing tools (e.g., SAST, DAST, SCA) to identify security vulnerabilities and code quality issues early in the development lifecycle, incorporating security gates and approval workflows to enforce security policies and compliance requirements before promoting code changes to production, and integrating with security information and event management (SIEM) systems and audit logging frameworks to monitor pipeline activities, detect anomalies, and maintain audit trails for compliance reporting and incident response.

Conclusion

In summary, "System Design Interview: 300 Questions and Answers - Prepare and Pass" serves as a comprehensive resource for individuals aspiring to excel in system design interviews. Throughout this book bundle, we have delved into various aspects of system design, covering fundamental concepts, advanced techniques, and practical strategies to tackle a wide range of interview questions.

From understanding scalability and distributed systems to designing for fault tolerance and security considerations, each chapter has provided invaluable insights into the intricate world of system design. Whether you are navigating through challenges in building scalable architectures, optimizing performance, or addressing emerging trends, this bundle equips you with the knowledge and tools necessary to navigate the complexities of system design interviews with confidence.

By combining theoretical knowledge with practical examples and real-world scenarios, "System Design Interview: 300 Questions and Answers - Prepare and Pass" empowers readers to enhance their problem-solving skills, critical thinking abilities, and decision-making capabilities. As you embark on your journey to mastering system design interviews, may this book bundle serve as your trusted companion, guiding you towards success and proficiency in the field of system design.

In closing, I extend my best wishes to all readers as they embark on their system design interview preparation journey. May your dedication, perseverance, and passion for learning pave the way for a fulfilling and rewarding career in system design.

www.ingramcontent.com/pod-product-compliance
Lightning Source LLC
Chambersburg PA
CBHW070937050326
40689CB00014B/3237